What inspires you

Doug - Caroline (my wife), Mia and Oli and every minute of everyday.

Geoff - People. Family and friends. Humility. Effort and enthusiasm. Great ideas. Deadlines!

Scott - Getting my teeth into a research project. Previously, I have managed large, international projects for a variety of clients.

Karl - Music.

Pete - Innovative people.

Natalie M - Sunshine, people, experiences, bravery, beauty, talent, my Gran.

Mike L - Scotland. Sporting achievement, especially British/Scottish. Things I could never do, like climbing Everest. Eric Liddell inspired me in the film, Chariots of Fire. Archie Gemmill. A wee, bearded, baldy guy can make an entire nation leap to its feet.

Caroline T - Nature, wildlife - feeling insignificant in the middle of a forest, savannah, or on a beach - where the experience and power of nature is so overwhelming with its beauty and diversity that it makes me really appreciate just being able to be.

The human body and mind, and its remarkable ability to move around in gravity with such ease and be able to overcome such incredible challenges...

Walking. African dance and music. Writers and travellers such as George Alagiah, Wilfed Thesenger, Nelson Mandela, Sally Morgan. People who overcome incredible challenges.

Toby - Extreme talent. People overcoming obstacles. Humility. A fear of losing.

Jon - My background (Barnsley), my roots, my partner Johane, my 2 kids, my mum and family, (particularly my grandad who is sadly no longer with us although somehow continues to inspire me everyday), winning! All aspects of design but particularly fashion and lifestyle. Life! I live life like a sponge - I believe you should never stop looking and listening, as soon as you do, you're finished! (You should see me trying to get around a supermarket!)

Clare - Freedom in all aspects of life.

Colin - Making sure the job that I do is done to a high standard and dealt with in a professional manner.

Bernie - Intelligent, down to earth, happy people; my 9 month old daughter when she smiles at me (sorry!); my wife when she is proud of me (sorry again!); Liverpool FC when they play inspirationally (very rare these days).

Richie - Words, Pictures, Music, My other half (no I'm not schizophrenic, I mean Suzanne) and learning the artistry of cooking - maybe Lance Armstrong but let's face it he's the new Greg Lemond, so I'd have to say the pair of them.

Ian - Listening to really crap, sad music from my generation.

Helen - My friends and family which I think are the two most important things in this life.

Delia - Money.

Andy I - Other people's work in all different types of media.

Dave - People who never accept the hand they are dealt.

Jen - Enthusiastic and passionate people.

Nick - Determined/focused people. Creative thinkers, the outdoors. Jake every morning.

Bart - River Thames and Jacqueline's laugh.

Justin - Friends.

Mark - London life.

John D - Seeing my children mastering walking, reading, writing and Super Mario Sunshine.

Ray - Ice-cream.

Malcolm - The great wide open...

Caroline B - The sunshine, happy people, visiting new places.

Craig - The things and people around me.

Natalie C - Mashed potato and gravy.

Rachel - My mum and dad, photography.

Jane - Happiness.

Rosie - Meeting interesting people.

John S - Wide open spaces/ideas.

Gavin - Life, Love and Liberty.

Liza - My mum, family, friends and of course my fella.

Stuart - Just life in general.

Paul - Tales of winning or survival against the odds.

Jonathan H - My mum.

Favourite place

Doug - Home.

Mike R - Skye.

John D - Glencoe - cos it's big and scary and awe-inspiring.

John S - You must go mountain bike wine tasting from Queenstown New Zealand around the Otaka vineyards.

Vic - Lagundry bay, Nias, Indonesia. Taking the overcrowded, overnight rickety wooden ferry from Sumatra, full of locals, goats, chickens and coconut oil to get there... (its all part of the experience) and once there: perfect barrelling waves surfable twice daily. No regular electricity or running water, no phones, no internet. Just an endless supply of perfect waves.

Geoff - The riverbank is my favourite place. Not a tow path or well trodden country walk - somewhere a little less manicured and wilder. The UK has some beautiful countryside. On my own and without a phone. One hour spent by the side of running water is equivalent to 10 hours of therapy!

Dave - Glencoe - Just has an atmosphere unlike any other place I've been.

Mike L - Tasmania. It was like a home from home with funny accents.

Toby - Any mountain, anywhere, above the clouds.

Caroline B - Any beach with clean sand and clear water and blue skies. Perfect.

Malcolm - Lanrick Castle, Near Doune.

Jane - Belongil Beach, Byron Bay.

Scott - The Treehouse, Georgetown, Grand Cayman - My fiancée and I had a lovely meal with our best friends, who now live in the Caymans. The table was situated on the end of a pier and we watched the sun go down and fed the fish while we softened plenty of cocktails.

Natalie C - Arriving in New York and going straight to Danni Tenaglia's birthday party at Vinyl then getting up the next day on a cold, sunny Manhattan morning and looking out my hostel window to the 'view', amazing city. Would recommend the helicopter ride over the lower east side of the city and going for a late night candle lit supper at (can't remember the name of the restaurant but can find out). If you want somewhere more original then sail a tall ship to the tiny Island of La Gomera off the African coast (one of the Canary Islands) and cook for 60+ inexperienced sailors in a gale force 9 for two weeks of the year, now that's an alternative break from the norm! (Especially when you meet your first love on board).

Pete - Cappadocia, Turkey - Magical landscape, brilliant people and the opportunity to sleep in a cave.

Jonathan H - San Francisco, Alcatraz, China Town, Golden Gate and the Streets.

Karl - Miners Arms Discotheque, Pinxton, Nottinghamshire - Lively to say the least.

Matt - Primrose Hill in London - for the view.

Jon - My home. The pub on Match day.

Favourite piece of music

John D - Chopin - Piano Concerto No 2, 2nd Movement.

John S - Bach cello concerto in b flat minor (I think).

Doug - The Clash - London's Calling.

Vic - Difficult to give just one but possibly the Kruder and Dorfmeister remix of Lamb's Transfattyacid.

Gavin - .Bring on the Clowns.

Geoff - That's so difficult. Music matches mood. However, if I was stuck somewhere for a long time (desert island disc) with one piece of music to play it would probably be 'classical'. Mozart's 4th horn concerto. (...it was the first album I ever bought! Can you believe it?).

Mike L - I love old stuff - Cat Stevens and new Stuff - the Chili Peppers.

Dave - The Flower Song from the opera Carmen.

Mike R - An Ending (Ascent) by Brian Eno.

Toby - Impossible. But 'We All Stand Together' by Paul McCartney and The Frog Chorus has to be right up there.

Caroline B - Roberta Flack, The first time I saw your face (is one of many faves).

Karl - Funnily enough, I was talking about this last night - with regards to what song I would have played at ... probably Kiss ... way in and Gr... the way out. ... of 'Rock n rol... that's not ver... 'Fox in the sn... Sebastian wo... Oh, I don't kn... BE original. A... is: 'Time to say goodbye' by Sarah Brightman and Andrea Bocelli - not very rock n roll, however, a beautiful epic of a song).

Bart - Gorecki by Lamb. Soaring!

Malcolm - Joy Division.

Jane - Too difficult!.... Nirvana, Smells Like Teen Spirit or REM, Everybody Hurts.

Pete - River man - Nick Drake.

Scott - "Step On" by the Happy Mondays or "I Am The Resurrection" by The Stone Roses ... summed up an age now gone.

Matt - Nirvana - Smells like Teen Spirit.

Jonathan H - Adagio for Strings - Samuel Barber (Platoon).

Natalie C - Somewhere over the rainbow (Eva Cassidy).

Favourite film

John D - Inherit the Wind - 1960-something, Spencer Tracy.

Mike L - The Great Escape, Deliverance, 12 Angry Men.

John S - The African Queen/ Ice cold in Alex/Dogtown and z boys.

Vic - Buffalo 66 (starring Vincent Gallo).

Gavin - Patch Adams.

Doug - Last of the Mohicans.

Geoff - The unrivalled - 'Carry on Screaming'.

Dave - A Matter of Life and Death.

Mike L - Deliverance.

Toby - The Big Lebowski.

Caroline B - Francis Ford Coppola's The Outsiders.

Bart - Bladerunner.

Malcolm - Banjo the Woodpile Cat.

Jane - Amelie.

Scott - "The Big Lebowski" or "O' Brother Where Art Thou?" by the Coen Brothers.

Natalie C - Big, Tom Hanks.

Matt - Oooh tough one - Star Wars, Spinal Tap or The Big ... n. ... one ... it a ... nge anybody to a 'we go together' lyrical showdown OR the 'Born to Hand Jive' bust a move dance contest - I'M NOT JOKING!!

Jonathan H - Raging Bull, Martin Scorsese film starring Robert De Niro and The Great Escape, John Sturges film starring Steve McQueen.

Jon - Loads but Gladiator takes some beating.

Favourite book

John - I am legend, by Richard Mathieson.

John S - Shigeo Fukuda - Shigeo Fukuda.

Vic - Ecclesiastes (The bible).

Doug - Tolkien - Lord of the Rings.

Gavin - The Return of the Prodigal Henri JM Nouwen.

Geoff - As a kid I had a morbid curiosity for horror stories. Edgar Allen Poe, The Pit and the Pendulum fuelled an early imagination.

Dave - The Third Policeman - Flann O'Brien.

Mike L - The Day of the Jackal by Frederick Forsyth.

Toby - Siddharta by Herman Hesse, The Secret History by Donna Tartt.

Caroline B - Michael Moore's Stupid white men.

Bart - Trainspotting.

Malcolm - Wired - the Short Life & Fast Times of James Belushi or The Railway Man by Eric Lomax.

Matt - A Thousand Years of Nonlinear History - Manuel Delanda.

Pete - Trophies - David Sylvian.

Jonathan H - Steve McQueen - An American Rebel, Marshall Terril.

Karl - I don't read that many books so I'd say Harry Potter One - It made me want to own a pet dragon and be a caretaker of a magic school.

itled 'A Child Called It', 'The Lost Boy' and 'A Man Named Dave'.

Dave - A matter of life and death.

Jane - Memoirs of a Geisha.

Favourite food

Scott - Chicken fajitas.

Karl - Cereal.

Pete - Thai Green Curry and Green and Black's Dark Chocolate.

Geoff - A chip buttie (plenty salt and vinegar) - (when I need one...) A Ruby Murray when I need one...) Steak anytime...).

Natalie M - Pasta, toasted muffins with smoked salmon & poached eggs, ice-cream, chips.

Mike L - Pasta, potato scones, haggis, hummus and Chorizo sausage.

Caroline T - Indian and Kenyan food.

Toby - Things in shells (but not snails), Chips (but not French fries), roast beef, Yorkshire pudding and gravy (but not Brussels sprouts).

Jon - Indian, Fish and chips in Yorkshire and my partner Johane's bacon and eggs.

Clare - My Nan's sunday lunch.

Colin - Chinese, Italian and good old steak!

Richie - Toad in the Hole, gravy, roast potatoes, maybe some honey roasted parsnip and some slices, not cut into discs, carrots. Or fish - any kind, seared and serve with new potatoes and salad.

Ian - Chicken Nentara.

Bernie - My mum's hot pot with red cabbage and tomato sauce.

Helen - Coronation Chicken with roasties made by mam Grimley.

Delia - A veggie burger and chips.

Andy I - Love all types of food.

Dave - Thai.

Jen - Fruit.

Nick - Indian (but not with whisky!)

Bart - Boullebaise (fish selection) in Corsica last summer.

Justin - I recently discovered the joys of pistachio nuts, after eventually getting over a nut allergy I realised I never had.

Rachel - Chinese.

Mark - Depends on mood. I love all food.

John D - Anything remotely resembling curry.

Ray - Mayo/cheese/peanut butter toasty.

Malcolm - Thai.

Caroline B - Mmmm - chocolate.

Craig – If I am cooking - Pasta! If Kate is cooking it is all lovely, if I know what is good for me!

Natalie C - Mashed potato & gravy.

Jane - Original Tim Tams, pancakes, Cheesels, strawberries, pasta.

Rosie - Sausage and Mash, Macaroni Cheese, Christmas Dinner, Potato Waffles, Chocolate... too many to list them all...

John S - Buttered toast and custard (not together).

Mike R - Toast and Bovril.

Gavin - Hot spicy anything.

Liza - Anything Chinese.

Stuart - Steak.

Jonathan H - Mince & Potatoes and Stovies.

Paul - Something with a bit of spice.

Favourite drink

Scott - Appletise.

Karl - Strongbow.

Pete - Coffee.

Natalie M - Champagne/ diet coke/sparkling water.

Mike L - Probably white wine. Very cold. Wouldn't say no to a cheeky malt whisky either.

Caroline T - Red wine in Europe, beer and passion fruit juice in the tropics, my cup of tea in the morning.

Toby - Coke for a buzz (I'm not good with e numbers), Gin and Tonic for a sunny day (few things more relaxing than a glass or two of Gentleman's Refresher), Good red wine for a special occasion (out of the biggest glass possible), Champagne for an excuse (any excuse). Port for the end of the evening (and for a proper hangover).

Helen - Cosmopolitans and tea (pantone ref 465).

Bart - Elderflower champagne the way me mum made it.

Jon - Beer (particularly Peroni and Cobra), Port and a nice cup of tea!

Clare - Shandy Bass, Dandelion & Burdock.

Colin - Tea, the odd beer or a glass of port.

Richie - Depending on the type of day this varies from a nice brew to Stella Artois.

Ian - Rum 'n' milk.

Bernie - Lager.

Delia - Wine.

Andy I - Irn-Bru.

Dave - Tea.

Jen - Tia Maria & Coke.

Nick - Lagavulin 16 yr malt whisky.

Mark - Vodka and Lemonade.

John D - Hobgoblin Ale.

Ray - Cremola foam.

Malcolm - Tequila & Ginger Beer.

Caroline B - Home-made fruit juice & beer (not together though).

Craig - Guinness and when Helen is making the tea.

Natalie C - Southern comfort and fresh orange followed closely behind by Petit Chablis.

Rachel - Vodka.

Jane - Gin & Tonic.

Rosie - Gin & Tonic.

John S - Water.

Mike R - Tea.

Gavin - Shiraz.

Liza - Baileys with ice, cocktails and strawberry milkshakes.

Stuart - Pepsi and Stella.

Jonathan H - Guinness.

Paul - Must be coffee as I drink a bucket load a day, even though I never make any.

Any other favourites

Clare - Being daft and loud.

Scott - Chicken Szechezuan (is that how you spell it?)

Pete - My Parker Fly classic (cherry red finish) and my trusty Boss DR55.

Colin - Football, Golf.

Karl - Nothing from Zinc as it gives me food poisoning.

Jon - Shopping (clothes and interior/lifestyle items).

Geoff - I've probably got a favourite something or someone in every 'category' in the world. Too much to mention. I like a lotta things.

Natalie M - Jelly Tots, shoes, shopping, Harvey Nicks, Jimmy Choo.

Caroline T - Steve - my partner, my family, my dog - Tom. My godchildren and my niece and nephews.

Toby - Muhammad Ali, Vince Lombardi, James Hunt. The Big Lebowski, The Godfather, One Flew Over The Cuckoo's Nest.

Richie - Middlesbrough FC, Kylie, A Nice Brew, Peter Kay, Championship Manager, Driving Cars Fast.

Ian - Time of day-between 2am and 3am, when I sleep.

Bernie - Anything fried.

Helen - Shoes and handbags, my dream to own a pair of Jimmy Choo's before I die!

Delia - Pasta.

Andy I - Too many to mention.

Dave - Derby County.

Jen - Chocolate and learning languages.

Nick - Too many to list.

Bart - Cheesecake/Liverpool FC exploring London/slagging off adverts on sofa with Jac/Sunday evenings/Monkey Dust/6ft under/Shameless.

Justin - Putting slinky's on escalators in Selfridges.

Mark - Music and the ladies...

John D - Sheepies and goaties. And Wagner.

Ray - Midnight snacks.

Malcolm - 3, Yellow, Albinoni's Adagio in C Minor, Jack Russel.

Caroline B - NewYork City, girly nights out, swimming in the sea, Saturday mornings, long hot baths, summer holidays, loud music, internet shopping, breakfast in bed.

Craig - Shortbread.

Rosie – The summer.

Rachel - Travelling, shopping and Madonna.

Natalie C - Corn on the cob with or without mash. Bridies are mingin' but I'll mention them anyway.

John S - Favourite places - The top of Farelton Knot, Cumbria.

Mike R - James Bond.

Gavin - more hot spicy anything!

Liza - Apple pie with ice cream, pretzels, pizza, chips and King Prawns oh and donuts too!!!

Stuart - Pizza.

Jonathan H - Summer holidays.

Paul - I quite like the feeling when you wake up in a nice warm bed and it's nasty weather outside.

Transport

Scott - Bike... My only consistent form of exercise.

Karl - Depends what happens... On a bad day... District line to Earls Court, Piccadilly Line to South Kensington, Circle line to Victoria, Victoria Line to Kings Cross and finally Metropolitan Line to Barbican!!

Pete - Anything that gets me home for "bath time" will do nicely.

Geoff - Tube, Taxi and Tank (Automatic armour plated 4x4). Its the only way to travel in London. However, if I had the chance the older Aston Martins would take some beating.

Natalie M - A BMW 320 Convertible (something smaller may help improve my parking ability)! A chauffeur may be an even better solution.

Mike L - My Jeep Cherokee. Or my wife's Mini Cooper. I used to have a Triumph TR6 which was great. I'll own another one day.

Caroline T - Really appreciate the variety which we use to get all around the world and my faithful legs for carry me around.

Toby - Two rather short legs and a Mini Cooper.

Jon - Audi A8 4.2 Quatro Sport.

Paul - I would like to finish my Private Pilots License which I got half way through before my mortgage got in the way. In the meantime Ill make do with my BMW 325tds.

Clare - Legs, Taxis, Mercedes ML 320.

Colin - Morse mobile.

Richie - Imagination, or a VW Golf GT Tdi.

Ian - Volvo (for now), the future... who knows?

Bernie - Lifts off my mates who drive better cars than me.

Helen - 'Terrance' the silver Corsa.

Delia - Public.

Andy I - ?

Dave - Bicycle.

Jen - (do you mean how I travel to work? If so, by bus).

Nick - Saxo VTR.

Bart - Bike and clapped out Toyota ('gift' from mate).

Justin - I used to ride my bike. It was called the phantom. It cost £150. I rode it 4 times. then the wheel was nicked. I now walk.

Mark - Train.

John D - I drive because I have to. I like walking more.

Ray - Legs? Feet?

Malcolm - Sledging.

Caroline B - Touchy subject - have given my car to one of my buddies for the next 5 weeks (can't drive with a broken wrist!).

Craig - Planes, trains and automobiles.

Natalie C - No.16.

Rachel - My Grandad's motorbike.

Jane - Horse.

Rosie - Bus - still trying to pass my test!

John S - Bicycle.

Mike R - Feet.

Gavin - legs.

Liza - Purple Ford Ka - very chic - you can usually hear the music blaring from the car before you even see it.

Stuart - By car (Punto).

Jonathan H - Anything goes!

navyblue

navyblue

Conway Lloyd Morgan

avedition rockets

Imprint

Concept
Conway Lloyd Morgan

Editors
Petra Kiedaisch, Vineeta Manglani

Design and Art Direction
Navyblue Design Group
www.navyblue.com

Production
avcommunication GmbH, Ludwigsburg
Gunther Heeb

Printed by
Leibfarth & Schwarz, Dettingen/Erms

ISBN 3-89986-013-6
Printed in Germany

avedition GmbH
www.avedition.com

Bibliographic information
published by Die Deutsche Bibliothek

Die Deutsche Bibliothek lists this publication in the
Deutsche Nationalbibliografie; detailed bibliographic
data are available in the Internet at http://ddb.de.

Does it have to be 160pp?

contents

When you see this symbol turn to the page number indicated (in this instance page 94) to conclude the particular story

When you see this symbol turn to the endpapers at the front and back of the book

so where is navyblue?

Robert Main & Sons
202 Bruntsfield Place
+44 131 229 1727

Leith Walk Barbers
280 Leith Walk
+44 131 553 4538

It is a cold February morning and the piper by the Waverley Bridge labours unenthusiastically into “Fiddler’s Joy”, while “Too Long in that Condition” might be more appropriate.
In Tollcross the fishmonger completes a display of golf ball shaped haggis in his window, while the chip shop across the street is stocking up the Mars bars to be deep-fried that evening.
In Leith Walk a barber sets out the sign “Hot Turkish Shave”, while the bookseller a few doors down places in the window a selection of titles on 18th century France: no need of more to remind the discerning reader of the Auld Alliance.
The vendors of kilts and malts glance down the Royal Mile in search of tourists, even in this dull season. The flag on the Royal Bank of Scotland’s head office is particularly bright this morning – they have just declared a profit of over six billion pounds. By Holyrood House work continues on the new Scottish Parliament building, its costs rising in parallel to the walls. In the King’s Buildings an Australian graduate student waiting for the centrifuge pours a cup of tea, unaware

that the Edinburgh blenders who made it are about to close. In a pub in the Lawnmarket the bar staff set out the furniture and polish glasses in hushed, distraught voices – Scotland has just been beaten by Wales and at football, even. In the Scottish Executive building on Commercial Quay a civil servant redrafts a sentence, thinking his English colleague in the Home Office may not grasp the subtleties of "outwith". In Navyblue's office a worker checks her mid-morning cup of tea against a colour chart: a drop more milk to get to Pantone 465 and that will be perfection.

Snapshots of Edinburgh do not make a portrait of a city, far less of a country like Scotland. That much is obvious. But the image of city and country are, in this case, relevant, since Scotland has been defining itself through images even before George IV donned a kilt during his official visit in 1816. These images have worked at various levels: through painting and later photography and film, through literature, poetry and travelogues, through engineering, architecture and design. Not that the imagery has been in any way uniform: in a run reaching from the Waverley Novels to Whisky Galore to Trainspotting, homogeneity is hardly likely. But there are common features: a certain practical bent, a mental rigour (sometimes shading into dourness), a romantic twist and so on.

In the last decade or so the image of Scotland has changed further and changed faster. In the mid-1990s Scotland was diverse, disenfranchised and dependent on the distant goodwill of Westminster. This distance was an advantage in the longer term, in fostering the spirit of independence and difference that was to be rewarded when the 1997 election secured the referendum on a new Scottish Parliament. The event that perhaps marks the start of the progression was the nomination of Glasgow as European City of Culture and the discovery that the city on the Clyde was not entirely dreich and drunken. And films – particularly Braveheart in 1995 – also began to convey a different image.

In Mel Gibson's treatment of William Wallace the notion of the romantic chieftain was reinvented for a new generation, just at the time when disgust was growing with a relentlessly global view. Most importantly of all, however, the final establishment of a Scottish Parliament gave a new emphasis to the concepts of national identity and common purpose. (For the purists, of course, the first of July 1999 was not the official opening of a new Parliament but the resumption of a sitting interrupted in 1707).

If there is such a thing as the Scottish character, it does not reside in the barefoot, blue-faced Braveheart warrior any more than in the scheming skipper of Para Handy or the moody, dysfunctional but determined Inspector Rebus. These are all fictions and made to fictional ends. Independence – now more of a reality – is a better measure and an apt one too. It represents a different perspective on convention and fashion, a willingness to change and an attitude of planning ahead.

The Navyblue design consultancy started in Leith, the port of Edinburgh, in 1994. Four years later one of the founders, Geoff Nicol, moved south to start an office in London and has since built up its independent roster of clients, the two offices making a partnership rather than a hierarchy. "From the start", Doug Alexander, co-founder with Nicol, has explained, "we wanted to create a design consultancy, not a freelance outfit and so find somewhere that would give off the right ambience. And we always wanted to be partners with our clients. We don't have a house style and we don't employ "stylists" – nor for a long time did we have account handlers". Many other design companies pay homage to the concept of client as partner but at Navyblue this means that the first person a client meets is a designer – either one of the founders or a design director and from there the team is built up around the requirements of the job. "We hope this is the beginning of a strong relationship between the client and the team. From that emerges a solid piece of work, which delivers something for the client, because the client has been involved in the process. What we have done is to build the skill base that articulates the client's needs". Thinking in team terms and along client-led ways means forgetting traditional distinctions between media, as many other design companies have discovered: "I can't remember the last time I used the term "graphic designer" in a presentation", Alexander observed. And as Nicol has pointed out, "from the start we aimed to be a multi-skilled company working from a multiple range of locations".

So saying that Navyblue is a "Scottish" design consultancy is not accurate geographically, nor in terms of their client base, nor of the composition of their design teams. Yet the company's rise to recognition parallels in some way the increasing response to Scotland of the last decade and its spirit of thinking out louder matches much in the Scottish character. So perhaps Navyblue is not in Scotland, Scotland is where it comes from.

what does navyblue mean to you?

IBM logo designed
by Paul Rand

"No-one ever got sacked for buying Big Blue" was a marketing mantra of the 1960s, when IBM – Big Blue from the colour of its logo – dominated the business computer market. The word blue has many layers of meaning: in music, authentic, passionate, creative, for example, while in imagery pornographic, false and faked. Natural colour of ocean and sky but there are no blue foods (not even the grass for those Kentucky racehorses). The pigment ground from lapis lazuli that was the most expensive ingredient in mediaeval art – dearer than gold – or the patented IKB so special to Yves Klein shows blue as a continuing force in art.

What one is not is no definition of what one is. What a name might mean is more that what is in a name. Calling a design group blue is an invitation to enquire, to experiment, to experience. The name Navyblue is exclusive without too much exclusion, inclusive without fixed limits, a name to be known by, not limited to.

what does navyblue
mean to you?

pantone 281

actually it's C 100%, M 72%, Y 0%, K 38%

what does navyblue
mean to you?

Miles Davis, Kind of Blue
Columbia Records 1963

Photography: Phil Thornton Tel: +44 131 620 0341

Just Girls, February 2004
Jerry's corner shop, Leith

what does navyblue
mean to you?

Photography: Colin Grey Tel: +44 141 334 4020

Boneyard Tattoo
177 Constitution Street, Leith
+44 131 467 7011

(No appointment necessary)

so where did the name come from?

Myths surround the origin of the name Navyblue

Here are three

Take your choice

so where did the name come from?

Photography: Euan Myles Tel: +44 131 659 5445

Shirt, T, short sleeve, Mark 1, white: standard issue for American troops in the European theatre in World War Two, the T-shirt was a lot cooler, in all senses, than the vest, cellular, khaki issued to British troops. Underwear became outerwear in cult films such as Streetcar Named Desire, on the person of Marlon Brando and later on Jean Seberg in Breathless. T-shirt becomes fashion. Today it is probably the commonest, most universal item of clothing in the world, familiar to everyone and yet capable of infinite variation and personalisation. Wear it to support your favourite band, shout your favourite slogan, stand up for your favourite team. In white, in red, in your favourite colour.

Navyblue is the world's favourite colour, research says, so the name Navyblue was chosen because it has a similar abstract and universal quality. Like a T-shirt, in fact: endlessly adaptable, never out of fashion.

so where did the name
come from?

MARION VOY

Psychic Readings
Clairvoyance, Tarot
Chakra Cards

For Individual or Group Bookings
www.mvoy.co.uk
01875 615 667
57 Briarbush Road, Macmerry

SHEILA SMITH

Or maybe that's not the right explanation. It seems that Geoff Nicol, one of the founding partners, went to see a fortune teller around the time the agency was being set up. Whether this was out of curiosity, conviction or just as a lark, history does not relate. Nor does it say whether the time-worn phrases about dark strangers and love life were mentioned.

But the medium did say the words, "Don't worry. You are going to be safe. You have an aura around you. It's a blue aura and that means safety". Geoff and Doug were trying to decide on a name at the time – better not tempt fate. (When I first heard this story I smiled, then remembered that some years ago an American design director had read my palm – without my asking her to, as it were – and came up with some oddly perceptive conclusions about me, even though we had never met before. So perhaps the story was not so surprising).

so where did the name
come from?

Then there is the third explanation, more down to earth. The new agency needed studio space. Leith, the port of Edinburgh, was accessible and inexpensive. In Leith, not surprisingly, there was a Maritime Lane, where the new team found space to rent. From maritime to navy to Navyblue was just a stroke or two away.

And perhaps all the stories are true. It is often the case that the precise reasoning behind a decision is not clear immediately, and less so with hindsight and in different voices. All the stories, however logical, however magical, might be true, each in its own way. And what matters is not so much where a name comes from, as what a name means.

who are navyblue then?

"Diversity is what keeps it together" has been said of many creative teams, not just in design. But by diversity in design one does not just mean different specialities – illustration, typography, colour, planning, interior design and so on. A mixture of personalities, attitudes, experiences, sensibilities is also needed. If one team member claims as favourite reading the intellectual pyrotechnics of Manuel de Landa, another cites Harry Potter (presumably not a reference to the historian of Tudor Scotland). If some like cerebral films such as A Matter of Life and Death or Wings of Desire (both meditations on the angelic), others prefer something less demanding like Star Wars or even Carry On Screaming.

Navyblue designers' favourite places range from Glencoe ("big and scary and awe-inspiring"), to a riverbank (the wilder the better), to a disco in Nottinghamshire, a beach in Indonesia, or the former prison at Alcatraz in San Francisco Bay.

Their taste in music runs from Chopin's Piano Concerto no. 2 (the second movement specifically) via Scar Tissue by the Red Hot Chili Peppers to "Somewhere Over the Rainbow" (Eva Cassidy not Judy Garland), to the Kinks, Nirvana, Paul McCartney and Roberta Flack, plus S Club Seven and on to Bach and Mozart. Ask about a favourite drink and the answer can be anything from a cup of tea, to a specific 16 year old malt, to detailed instructions for a rum cocktail. For one person mashed potato and gravy is a favourite food, for another a source of inspiration. And other sources of inspiration include the River Thames, a baby daughter's smile, Barnsley, the explorer Wilfred Thesiger, cooking, money, deadlines, Liverpool Football Club and "listening to really crap sad music from my generation…"

Some of the comments are not quite serious, some of them wry, some of them surprising, all of them are enthusiastic. Many of the team also

Miners Arms Discotheque
Church St, West Pinxton
Nottingham
Nottinghamshire
NG16 6NB

Lagavulin, the classic Islay malt
16 years old, 43% volume

wanted specifically to work for Navyblue, some applying several times before being taken on. (One person immediately applied "after being warned by my friends against working there"). And once there they have a good time: favourite moments centre around parties and celebrations – not surprisingly, since they are a young team. (One person's worst moment at Navyblue was discovering that one of the directors was younger than him!).

Someone once described Navyblue as "wide boys who got lucky". It's not a very generous compliment – if compliment it is. It has a ring of truth in that there are plenty of other design agencies that seem to have been born middle-aged, while Navyblue seem to be enjoying themselves too much even when they are working. But wide boys don't work. And, yes, the word Navyblue use to describe their experiences and work most often is "great".

Adrienne: Receptionist
Edinburgh

Malcolm: Receptionist
London

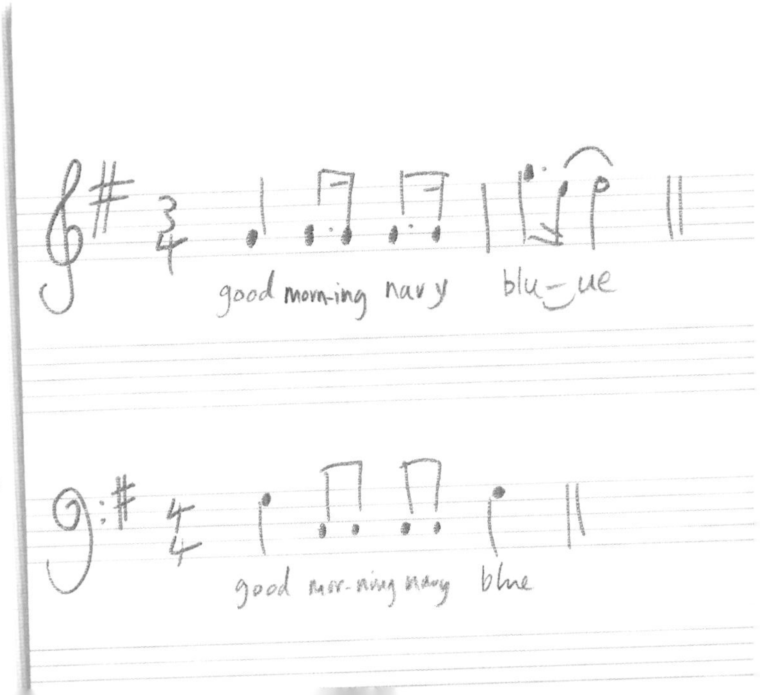

1 good morn-ing nav y blu – ue

2 good mor-ning navy blue

"Having walked through the door for the first time my gut reaction was... I could work there... I want to work there... I will work there"

Natalie, Senior Account Manager

You can't make a good apple pie out of bad apples!

Photography: Shannon Tofts Tel: +44 131 554 2154

John, Associate Design Director
toast with butter and jam

ingredients

Fresh granary or
wholemeal bread
Slightly salted Danish butter
Strawberry jam with lots of fruit

how to make it

1 Slice bread

2 Place in toaster

3 Depress lever and wait until it browns and pops up

4 Spread liberally with chilled butter

5 Apply strawberry jam as butter melts and slice in half horizontally

6 Serve immediately

Great with a cup of tea!

“Wide open spaces”

Douglas, Managing Director

Photography: Iain Stewart Tel: +44 131 453 4138

EP

"Music matches mood"

Geoff, Managing Director

Photography: Robbie Smith Tel +44 131 556 0345

EP

Photography: Robbie Smith Tel: +44 131 556 0345

"The greatest escape"

Toby, Client Services Director

EP

"It made me want to own a pet dragon and be a caretaker of a magic school"

Karl, Senior Designer

Photography: Robbie Smith Tel: +44 131 556 0345

04>

1 Geoff Nicol
Sons Alfie and Tate

2 Douglas Alexander
Daughter Mia and Son Oli

3 John Smart
Daughter Eve

4 Nick Needham
Son Jake

5 Pete Burns
Son Nate

6 Keith Blacklock
Daughter Poppy and Son Max

7 Jonathan Hope
Son Reece

8 Jonathan Evans
Daughter Amy and Son Liam

9 Bernie Shaw-Binns
Daughter Luisa

10 Ian Dixon
Sons Adam and Jack

11 Mike Lynch
Daughter Henrietta

12 Tim Sharp
Son Charlie

1

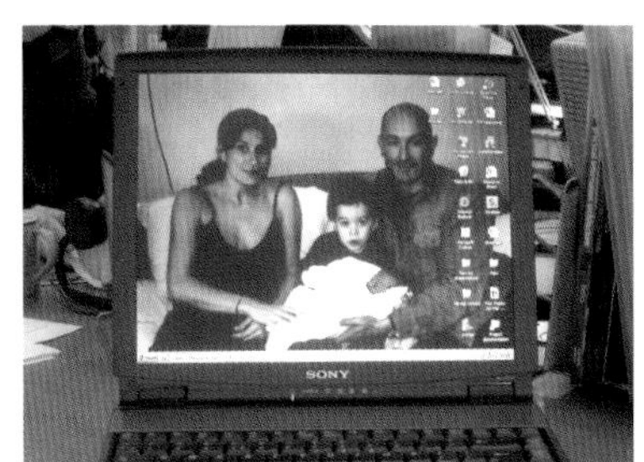

2

3

7

8

9

Photography: Phil Thornton Tel: +44 131 620 0341

"Until you become a parent it's difficult to imagine how rewarding it is"

Mike, New Business Director

4

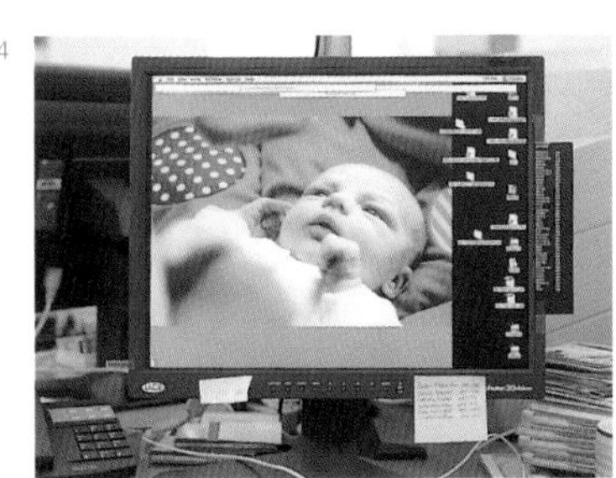

5

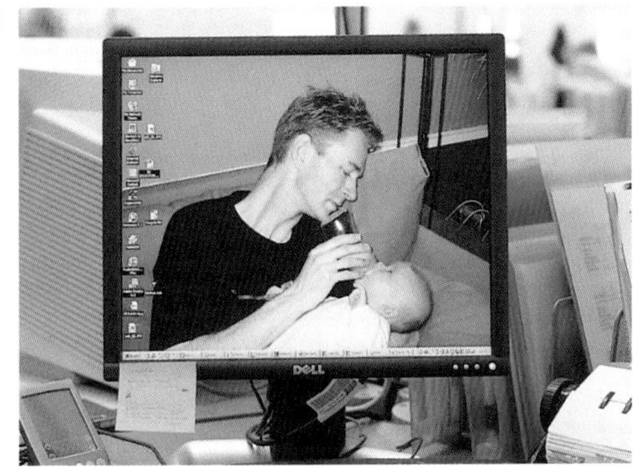

6

10

11

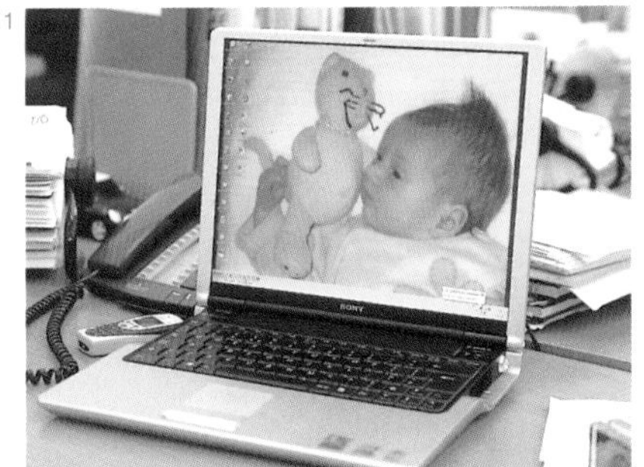

12

Photography: Euan Myles Tel: +44 131 659 5445

“Live life like a sponge – I believe you should never stop looking and listening, as soon as you do, you’re finished!”

Jonathan, Creative Director

EP

Teamwork Skills Client awareness Enthusiasm

so how do navyblue do it?

The blackboard outside the restaurant, a few yards from the Navyblue London office near the Barbican, announced the day's special: Carl's liver, green beans, onion mash. The apostrophe and the s made it clear this was a special special, not a commonplace eponym such as beef Wellington or veal Orloff. Perhaps the chef was called Carl (anyone else did not bear thinking about). Or perhaps it was a mishearing by a hurried signwriter.

Whatever the intent, a major communication failure. If it was a tasteless joke, then it was for a tasteless restaurant. If it was an error, what does it say about the place's care for detail and quality? If it was intended to highlight the chef, it put him in a poor light. Communication is not just a simple, two-way process and communication is at the heart of design.

Navyblue do not have a fixed recipe for design, still less a series of set dishes. There are some designers, and even agencies, that offer clients a certain style. If a pre-styled solution is what the client wants, that's fine. But talk to the team at Navyblue about their work and the word style hardly ever comes up.

The clients do come up, though: how one liked this idea, how another suggested that, how it seemed impossible to get so-and-so to accept such-and-such. Sometimes designers talk about clients as if there was an element of opposition in the relationship: not so at Navyblue. Not to say that there is not tension in the design process: after all, much – and not just expenditure – rests on a successful outcome. Looking back over the first ten years of the group's existence, Geoff Nicol points out that "we had to bring some clients along with us, others forced us to catch up on skills, many we worked with together in tandem". Getting close to the client, understanding their viewpoint, their needs, their language, has been a key to Navyblue's success.

If understanding the client is the first step, the next step – the creative one – is using that knowledge to exceed the client's expectations. This involves delivering better work than the client expected, or, more importantly, seeing further into the challenge and carrying that forward. The comments that Navyblue quote from clients regularly focus on this. "Navyblue challenged my perceptions of the work I expected them to deliver and exceeded them on all counts", said one. "We chose Navyblue for their ability to mould their structure to our needs, all the while challenging our thinking, approach and way of working", is another's comment.

To exceed expectations, Navyblue has to have a broad skills base. In a decade the group has built up from a purely graphics base to encompass three-dimensional work, including designing trade fair stands interpretating brands in three dimensions and retail work. Also an extensive portfolio of web work and other interactive design. Strategic planning, involved from an early stage, formally became part of the skills base in recent years. But skills are nothing without teamwork. For each project, an individual team is built up, depending on the tasks involved. Team structures are open, non-hierarchical, all contributions welcome.

Teamwork, skills and client-awareness are three key elements in the Navyblue offer. The final one is enthusiasm. Some design companies come across as serious, well-established, even formal, suited to the suits their clients presumably wear. Navyblue is distinctly different. The group's first strapline was "thinking out louder", and many insisted that the emphasis was on the loud! "I remember one designer, ending a presentation standing on his chair, he was so carried away", someone remarked "but we did get the job". "Clients have often said that our energy and eagerness was a deciding factor in our getting work", Geoff Nicol observes.

This partnership strategy between Navyblue and its clients can be seen in various ways: the way clients stay with the group is the obvious example. Others are more subtle: scattered through this book like appetisers are recipes for food and drink: most of them come not from designers but from clients. (And none contain liver, of any description).

We start with a blank sheet...

Kath Mainland: Unique Events
Water

Laurence Marzell: Amey
Coffee white

Kevin Bradley: Turner & Townsend
Tea milk two sugars

John Parker: Byrom
Coffee black

Charles McLeod: Amey
Water coffee black

Peter Irvine: Unique Events
Tea milk two sugars

Douglas Alexander: Navyblue
Water

Ronny Dool: Turner & Townsend
Coffee black one sugar

David Chudziak: Faber Maunsell
Coffee white

Jonathan Evans: Navyblue
One and a half croissants

Photography: Phil Thornton Tel: +44 131 620 0341

The joint decision by Scotland and Ireland to propose hosting the European Football Championship for 2008 can be compared to Japan and Korea hosting the 2002 World Cup, giving an international role to smaller nations. And giving the designers responsible for implementing the design, in this case, not one client but a locker-room full, starting with the Scottish Executive and the Irish Government and the two football associations. The challenge was to bring this client group together as a team around the table, so that they could go out together and convince the European authorities of the strength and validity of their bid.

This strategic role for designers in organising the planning and co-ordination of an issue rather than supplying the visual support for it seems surprising. This might be seen as a technical function, for managers and financial advisers. But a strategic approach comes out in the end as a matter of communication, both within the company to ensure everyone has the same goals and outside the company to clients and customers, regulatory authorities, the press and government and to shareholders. And in addition strategy is a task for generalists, not for specialists, or rather for those who can take a wider view. It is for these reasons that strategic work has become increasingly the province of design agencies. If this seems at first surprising, one need only think about the kind of issues that need to be addressed in creating a visual identity (how is the company perceived by its different audiences, what are the company's strengths and beliefs) to see how logical it is to extend this into general strategic work.

In Navyblue's case, their determination from the start to get closer to their clients and try and understand the whole of the client's situation and not just the content of the immediate brief, had them involved in thinking strategically from the first, though it is only in the last year that they have formally set up a strategy department.

66

Baxters are a traditional Scottish food producer, their soups and tinned goods, jams and marmalades being well established. They linked up with the Scottish chef, Nick Nairn, to create a premium range of food products that would offer restaurant quality food at home. Navyblue were asked to package the partnership. A conventional design approach would have looked to balancing the two names in some way but the Navyblue team, after extensive research into competing brands, decided that the right solution lay in emphasising the strengths of each – Baxter's reputation for goodness and quality combining with Nairn's flair and originality.

	£
RISOTTO	0.97
YELLOW THAI	1.64
RAITA	1.27
WINE/MROOM SCE	1.29
MAYONNAISE	0.95
BALLS CHUTNEY	1.45
INDIAN SAUCES	1.99
CHILLI SAUCE	0.94
THAI CURRY SAU	1.65
PATAKS CURRY S	1.41
PASTA SAUCES	1.60
ORGANIC SAUCE	1.79
DIPPING SAUCE	0.77
ORGANIC SAUCE	2.29
PASTA SAUCE	1.47
GRN LIME SAUCE	1.99
SUNDRIED TOMS	1.38
CHINESE SAUCES	0.99
PASTA SAUCE	1.09
STIRFRY SAUCE	0.46
COOKING SAUCES	1.16
CREOLE SAUCE	1.35
CURRY SAUCE	1.39
TOTAL	31.29

PUBLISHED TERMS AND CONDITIONS APPLY
Card Services Ltd. has handled this
Transaction for you for a fee of 2.5% included
In the cost of your shopping

** FOR INFORMATION ONLY **

YOU HAVE EARNED 3 COMPUTERS FOR
SCHOOLS VOUCHERS IN THIS TRANSACTION.

Collect vouchers in store until 02/05/04

28/03/04 11:49 2387 008 1207 1932

Tesco, Dalkeith, Midlothian

Nairns Cook School
Tel: 01877 385603

Photography: Iain Stewart Tel: +44 131 453 4138

Baxters
AND
Nick Nairn
sic Mediterranean Tomato Sauce
PAN FRY
CREATED BY NICK NAIRN FOR BAXTERS

WE CAN
DELIVER
Scotland and Ireland's Response
to the Schedule of Conditions for
the Host Associations
SCOTLAND
IRELAND'08

WE CAN
INSPIRE
Scotland and Ireland
A Glorious Celebration of the Beautiful Game
SCOTLAND
IRELAND'08

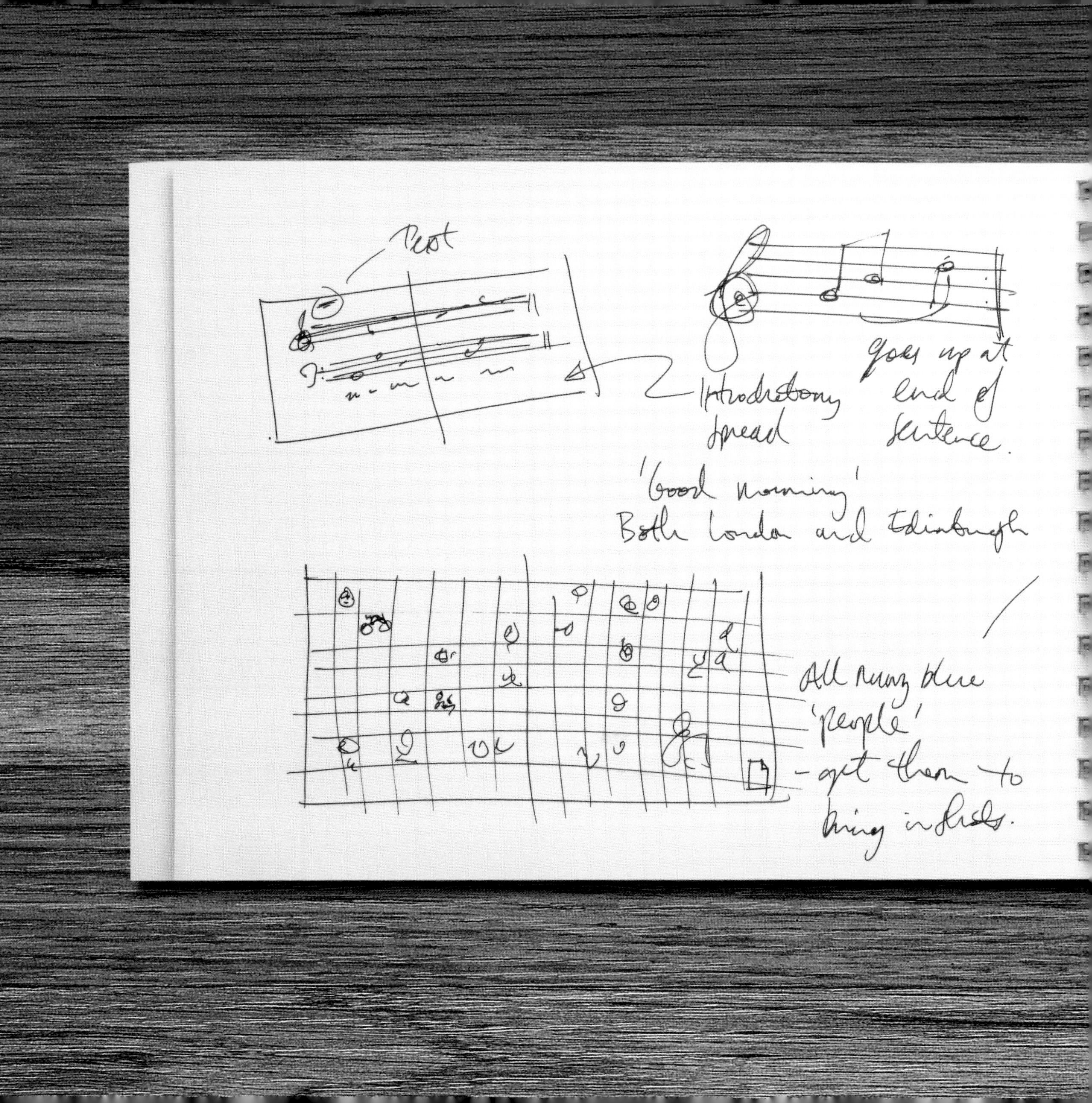

Rest

Introductory spread

Goes up at end of sentence.

'Good Morning'

Both London and Edinburgh

All very blue 'people' – get them to bring in [illegible].

Despite the ubiquity of the computer, the designer's first tool, in many instances is still the notebook. So a presentation notebook became a key element in the campaign Navyblue developed for Zanders paper, in which the key theme was ownership: my paper and so my notebook. Other parts of the campaign highlighted the paper's quality and versatility but a practical notebook was at the heart of it. Look around the Navyblue offices and there are plenty of them in use, as well. (Le patron dine ici, as the French restaurant signs used to say).

origin Greek in his o.
stamp of his lowly o.
original Behold the bright o.
gone from o. righteousness
great and o. writer
great O. frame
in th' o. perused mankind
nothing o. in me
ordinary one seem o.
o. face
o. is unfaithful
o. or instrumental
o. sin
o. writer
returning to the o.
saves o. thinking
To women their o. must owe
originality man without o.
o. of your countenance
originals do not admire the o.
few o. and many copies
origins Consider your o.
hands of O.

Photography: Douglas Jones Tel: +44 131 557 2200

Promotional work for paper manufacturers might seem like a soft option for a design studio. A wide brief, endless creative opportunity, a familiar medium – an opportunity to indulge.

In reality, this is business to business design with an edge: other designers may never see your packaging and identity work but they are the market paper promotions are intended for. So it is a challenge that requires self-criticism and an objective view to a high degree, as well as professional and creative skill. Would you keep your own work if it came in as a mail shot!

126

head in the clouds

Mobile phone operators Orange rewrote the rules about naming companies when they started some twelve years ago and they have continued to be innovative ever since. They work continuously to maintain and deliver their brand through their advertising, media work, sponsorship and retail outlets. But a brand has also to work internally, so Orange asked Navyblue's three-dimensional design specialists to help bring the company's brand and values into its workplaces, especially the call centres that are the hub of their connection to customers. "The key", one of the designers explained, "was stimulation, interactivity and inspiration. The work was all about emotional engagement, combining colour, imagery and language to bring the brand to life".

Getting within the Orange brand was equally important for the exhibition stand work Navyblue did for Orange. "Head in the clouds, feet on the ground" is a simple strapline but translating that offer of a mix of ambition and delivery into a visual reality required a deep understanding of the whole of the brand definition.

Ellesse Franco Fava shoe worn by
Bernie, Design Director

Photography: Phil Thornton Tel: +44 131 620 0341

Wearing the client's shoes is a phrase some Navyblue designers use to describe the importance of understanding the client's views and intentions. Seeing through the client's eyes might be a similar way of putting things, but the original phrase is absolutely right for Ellesse, a British-based makers of trainers and sports shoes. Ellesse have continually gained market share, thanks in part to the two and three-dimensional projects that Navyblue have designed for them, but also because of a decade of co-operation, shared ideas and experiences, between client and designer. What started as work on the seasonal catalogues that are Ellesse's main sales tool extended to cover the whole marketing demand from the company, which has since moved into the international arena.

Splashing through the surf in designer jeans is hackneyed advertising stuff. Getting soaked in the Firth of Forth because the photo was still not quite right while the tide was coming in is designer reality. The Scottish Arts Council had commissioned a series of posters and a website for their new music program, intended to bring in as wide an audience as possible, beyond "traditional music lovers". Putting musical instruments into everyday contexts would carry this concept but only if it was delivered with a maximum of realism and so it had to be that way, wet jeans or not.

Photography: Iain Stewart Tel: +44 131 453 4138

Craig's jeans

Photography: Phil Thornton Tel: +44 131 620 0341

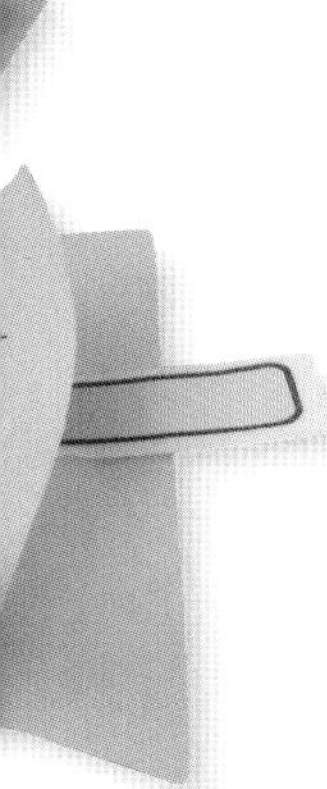

96

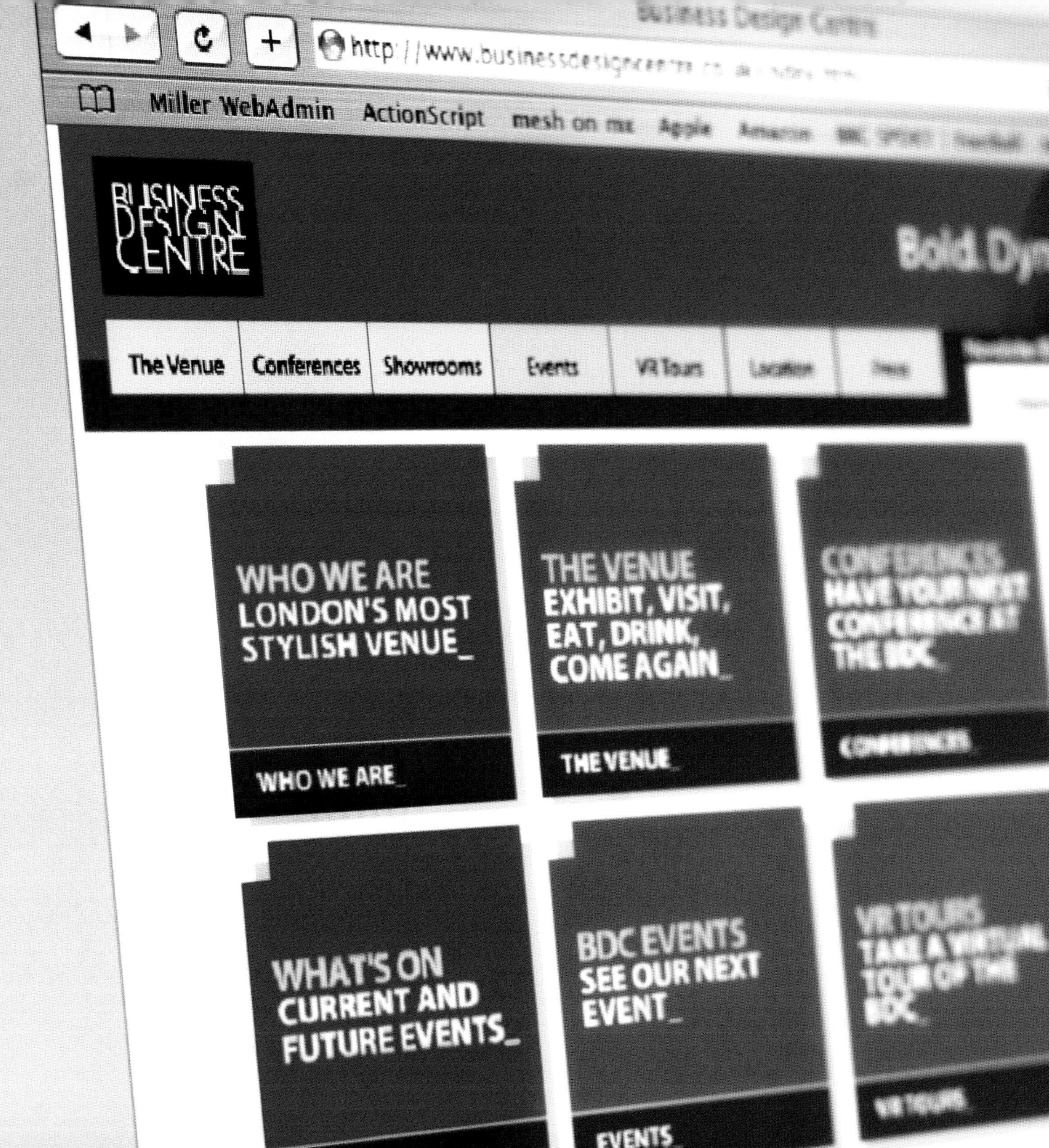

Photography: Stewart & Baxter Tel: +44 131 659 6262

www.businessdesigncentre.co.uk

The Business Design Centre in London is not just a conference centre, nor just an exhibition space but also a workspace for a number of independent companies and agencies. Its website needed to reflect this unique combination and position the Centre as somewhere “Bold, Dynamic, Central” and “Busy, Desirable, Contemporary”, straplines on the site that vary the acronym of the Centre. An additional feature is a virtual reality tour of the building that allows potential exhibitors to visit the place in advance.

Fiona Scott
Fiona Scott Communications
fish pie (inspired by Keith Floyd and Rick Stein)

ingredients

Highest quality, freshest fish you can get your hands on
1.5lb undyed smoked haddock
2 fillets lemon sole
1 fillet wild salmon
5 king prawns
5 scallops
2 shelled langoustine (for garnish)
1 peeled onion (studded with cloves)
1 bay leaf
1 pint semi skimmed milk
½ pint double cream
4 oz butter (Lurpak)
2 oz plain flour
4 hard boiled eggs
Home-made mashed potatoes
Chopped flat leaf parsley
Salt and black pepper
Nutmeg
Dill (for garnish)

how to make it

1 Poach all the fish (except langoustine) in the milk, cream, clove-studded onion and bay leaf
2 Bring to the boil and simmer for 8 minutes
3 Lift out the fish and strain juices into a jug
4 When cooled, flake the fish and place chunks in the bottom of a large ovenproof dish
5 Cut the hard boiled eggs in half and place randomly over the top of the fish
6 To make the sauce, melt the butter and flour into a paste, pour in the fish juices gradually and cook for 10 minutes, stirring all the time, then pour over the fish
7 Chill in the fridge for one hour
8 Top with home made mashed potatoes
9 Season with salt, black pepper and nutmeg and cook at 200ºC for 40 minutes
10 Serve piping hot with langoustine and dill as garnish, lots of crusty bread and a bottle of chilled Puligny Montrachet

Photography: Shannon Tofts Tel: +44 131 554 2154

"Edinburgh College of Art has a worldwide reputation, so it was always going to be a first place choice of study."

welcome to eca

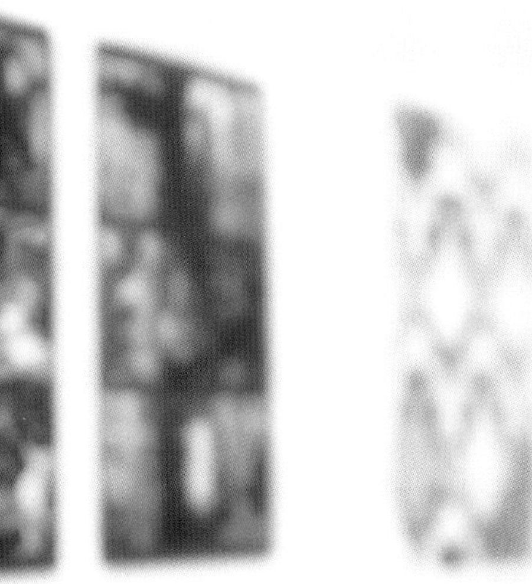

Photography: Nisbet & Wylie Tel: +44 141 226 3888

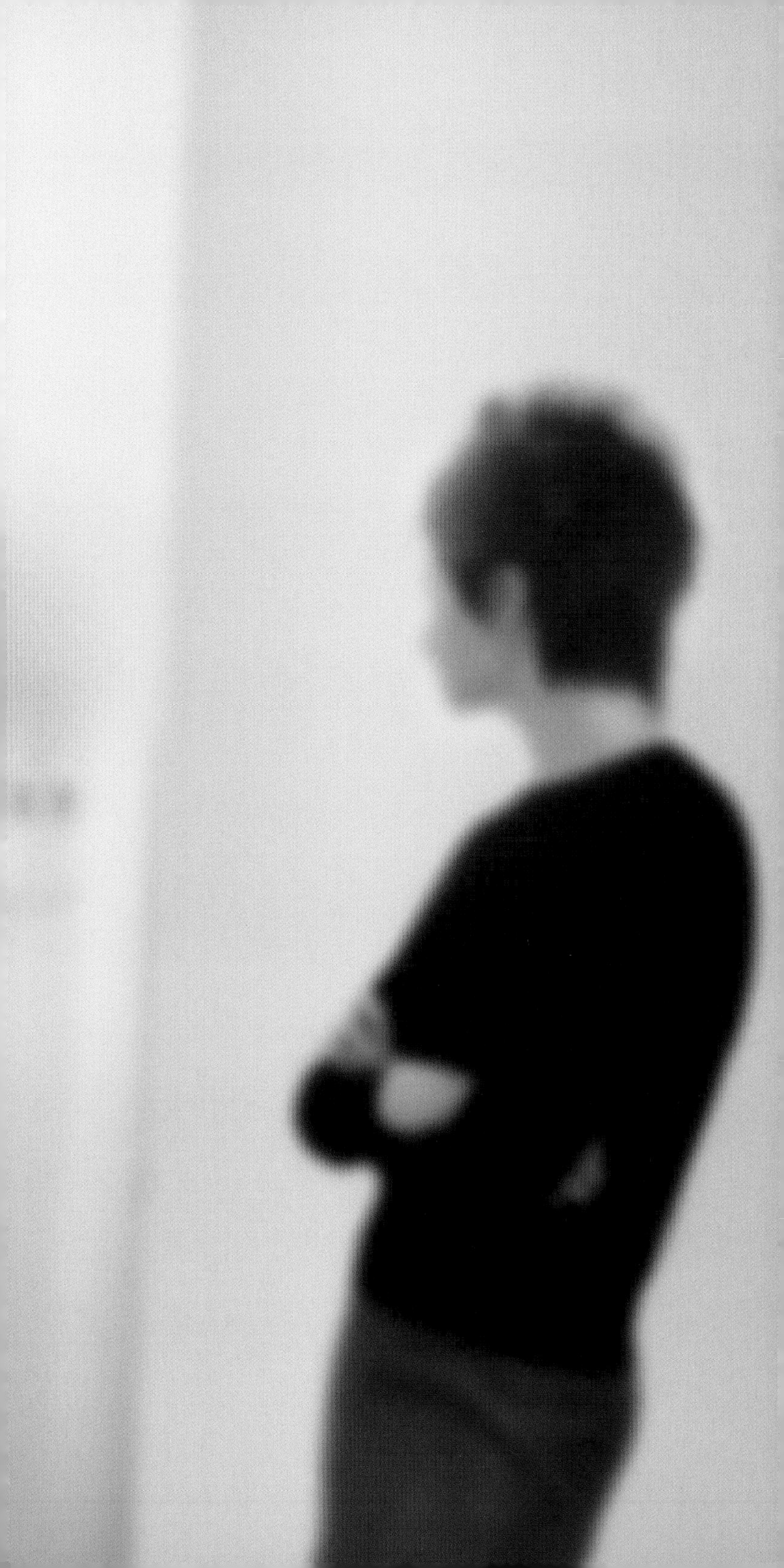

com/trains
CALEDONIAN 80/-
SHEPHERD + WEDDERBURN
GUINNESS
edinburghrugby.com

FGH

Having the party first and publishing the book it launches afterwards makes sense, when you also have a parrot called Jesus and two conversing light fittings. Navyblue had published two successive and successful, calendar books for papermakers Robert Horne and the third was to celebrate their new identity design. Images of the party and a narrative set in the party location were intertwined with brand statements in a loose-leaf publication featuring a range of different papers and cards. The result is a collaged multi-level jigsaw that celebrates design, paper and the client's role in the design world. And it must have been quite a party as well…

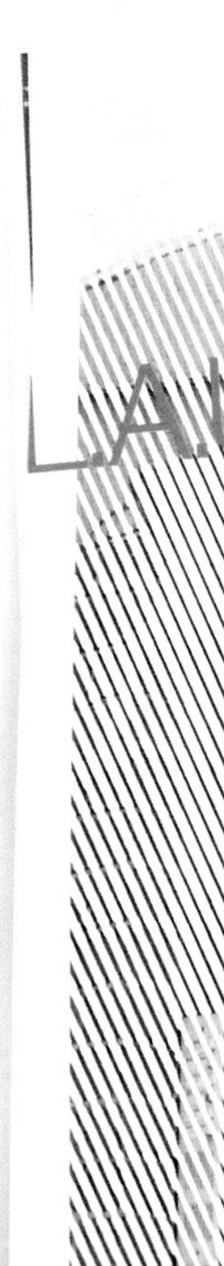

L.A.U.N.C.H. —08 OCT
—08 OCT 2002
7.30PM –1.00AM
BOOK
LASER SHOW
IDENTITY
SCULPTURE
DJ
CINEMA
FREE DRINKS
PARROT
INVITATION
ROBERT HORNE/FULMAR
NAVYBLUE
NICK REYNOLDS
MICK MARSTON
STRANGE SAVOY
LEE MAWDSLEY
TARDIS INTERNATIONAL
54 TURNMILL STREET
CLERKENWELL
LONDON EC1M 5QR
PLEASE RSVP ASAP
RACHEL.DAVISON@
ROBERTHORNE.CO.UK

104

Photography: Douglas Jones Tel: +44 131 557 2200

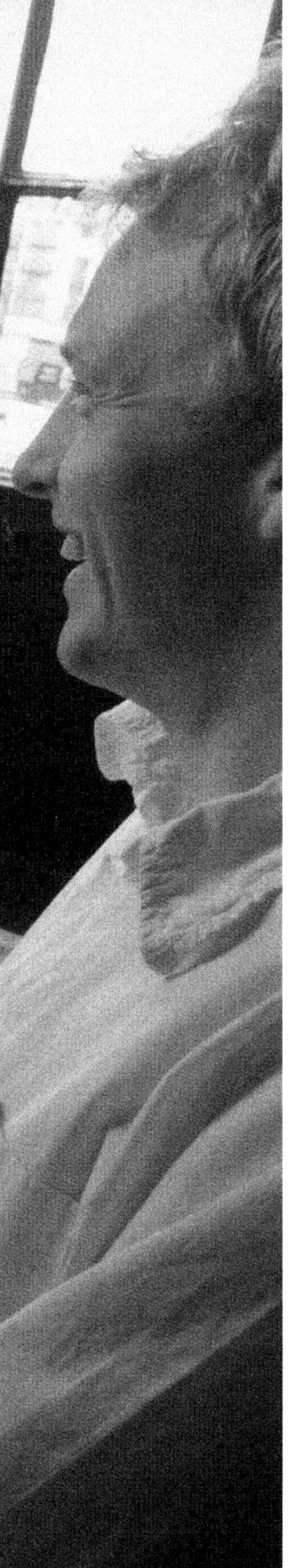

Great fish 'n' chips

King's Wark
36 The Shore, Leith
Edinburgh
EH6 6QU
+44 131 554 9260

There is a classic Navyblue story about the team going out to lunch with clients and getting so deep into talking they forget to order food. For the Bond advertising agency, it was a meeting in the pub. Navyblue had created the original identity for this break-away agency and the briefing for the website "took place in the King's Wark, as I recall", says Tim Sharp. The site is almost purely verbal, so resolving the conundrum of how to see the agency's personality underneath the work they have produced for their clients. And the tone is as direct, friendly and unsparing as a pub conversation can be.

100

The English National Opera was founded with two main aims, to bring opera to a wider public by singing in English and to provide performance opportunities to younger singers. The company built a reputation for quality and originality, commissioning new opera and staging innovative productions. At the start of the new millennium they also secured funding to renovate their London home, the Coliseum in London. They chose this as an opportunity to refresh their identity and market position and invited Navyblue to work on this with them. Navyblue recommended a new look, more direct and vibrant, even less polite, that would reflect ENO's engagement both with tradition and the avant-garde. This was to run across their posters, the seasonal brochures, the magazine and a new website, using contemporary typography and more editorial images. The website proposal would enable customers to book seats online and also listen to excerpts from productions (though this was not finally implemented). It was important for Navyblue and the client that the result be flexible and simple and work effectively across a range of media, to help build the ENO brand.

The 13.43 to Waterloo

243
VLW178
ENO
"AN EVENING TO RAISE THE SPIRITS" EVENING STANDARD
10 PERFORMANCES ONLY
THE BARBER OF SEVILLE
ROSSINI
SUNG IN ENGLISH
ENGLISH NATIONAL OPERA
AT THE LONDON COLISEUM
ST MARTIN'S LANE WC2
FIRST TIME TO ENO? CHECK OUT
WWW.ENO.ORG/FACT_FICTION
OCTOBER 24 TO NOVEMBER 28
BOOK NOW 020 7632 8300
WWW.ENO.ORG

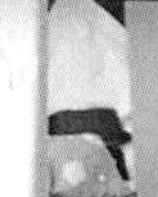

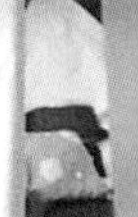
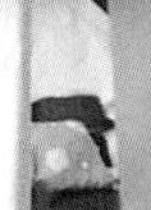

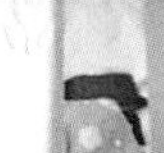

Photography: Colin Grey Tel: +44 141 334 4020

The study, Craig's girlfriend's mum and dad's house

Originally founded in 1947 but incorporating a wealth of other imagery from earlier times among its 15 million pictures, the Hulton Getty picture library is a major visual resource. In recent years they have worked with Navyblue to develop a number of promotional items intended to remind designers of the strength, depth and potential of the collection. Something that other photo libraries had previously failed to do. Each of these individual projects is interesting in itself but what the work with Hulton Getty shows overall is the depth of skill that enables a design group to come back to the same themes and still find new and original solutions.

Photography: Colin Grey Tel: +44 141 334 4020

78

orange
partner
REPSOL YPF
REPSOL YPF
EUROBET
EUROBET

72

Photography: Stewart & Baxter Tel: +44 131 659 6262

www.bondadvertising.com

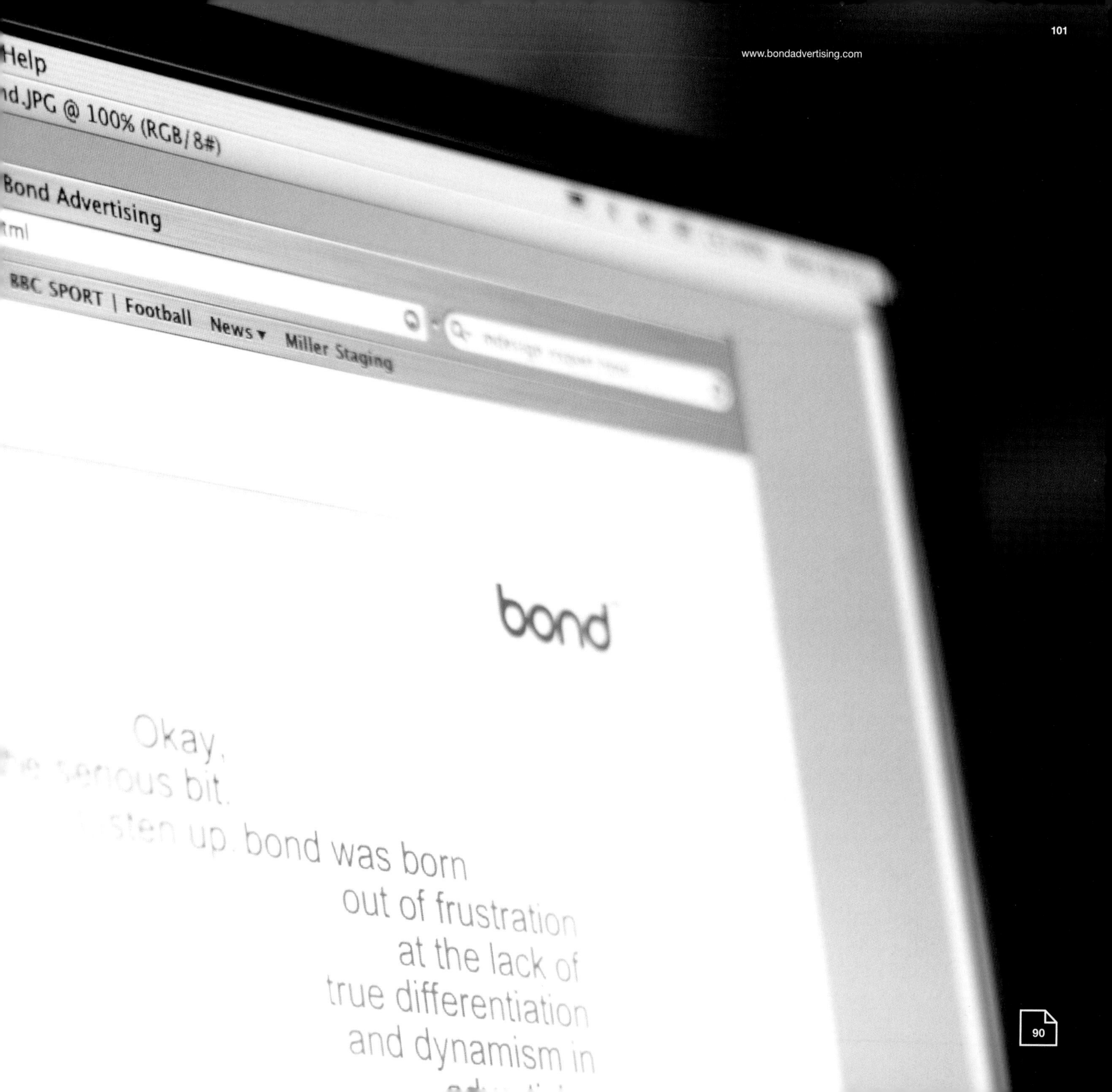

90

Victoria Turton
Bank of Scotland
chocolate brownie

ingredients

375g soft unsalted butter
375g best quality
dark chocolate
6 large eggs
1 tablespoon vanilla extract
500g caster sugar
225g plain flour
1 teaspoon salt

how to make it

1 Preheat oven 180ºC/gas mark 4

2 Line brownie pan with foil
or parchment

3 Melt the butter and
chocolate together

4 Beat the eggs with sugar
and vanilla

5 In a bowl mix flour and
salt together

6 When the chocolate has melted,
let it cool then beat in the eggs
& sugar and then the flour

7 Beat together until smooth

8 Put in the lined pan

9 Bake for 25 minutes

10 When done the top should be
dried to a paler brown speckle
but the middle dark and gooey

11 Leave to cool

12 EAT THEM

Photography: Shannon Tofts Tel: +44 131 554 2154

Mmm!

Photography: Stewart & Baxter Tel: +44 131 659 6262

LAUNCH + SCULPTOR
Playing with God
LAUNCH + GUESTS
The Objective
Some of these things are believed to have magical powers, and I think I heard that they even house a spirit.
Well, I tend to grasp the life-like presentations with a dispassionate view. They have an inaudible undertone, but somehow obvious, recognisable. A feeling of having previously undergone an experience that I am having now for the first time. I almost belong here.
Verity Strange, what is
I bet for the life of me
is true.
did Verity go? I don't know.

88

brightgrey:
We think bright, we act bright. In a grey times, we will be a source of warmth. We will lead the market, illuminating the way forward.
bright grey™
Grey times.
(IFA/BG ISSUES)
what are you waiting for? phone us 0845 6094 500
con trasts
BRIGHTGREY
brig
light and airy
brightgrey
BRIGHTGREY
personality
bri ht
BRI HT
contemporary
BRIGHTGREY
BRIGHTREY
news
Make health insurance compulsory
Delay to start of FSA regulation
in brief
77% say no to "simplified" sales
NHS needs to end long stays
friday
'phew! I'm glad I called Bright Grey'
phone us 0845 6094 500
discover for yourself what makes Bright Grey different
bright grey
advertising
campaigns
contact us
(we're friendly, efficient and ready to make you more profi
contact us
countdown
BRIGHTREY.
glowing
bright grey
caring
sensory
BRI HT
enveloping
emerging
bright grey™
bright grey
think bright
act bright
USB DRIVE
LESS IS MORE.
GUARANTEE -
SURE THAT THE SUN WILL
RISE AND SET
TARGETED
DM
(EXISTING)
SEEING
THINGS
DIFFERE
we will:
show real people real situations, creating intrigue with the everyday.
be clear and simple - let the picture tell the story
black and white is fine too, when it makes sense

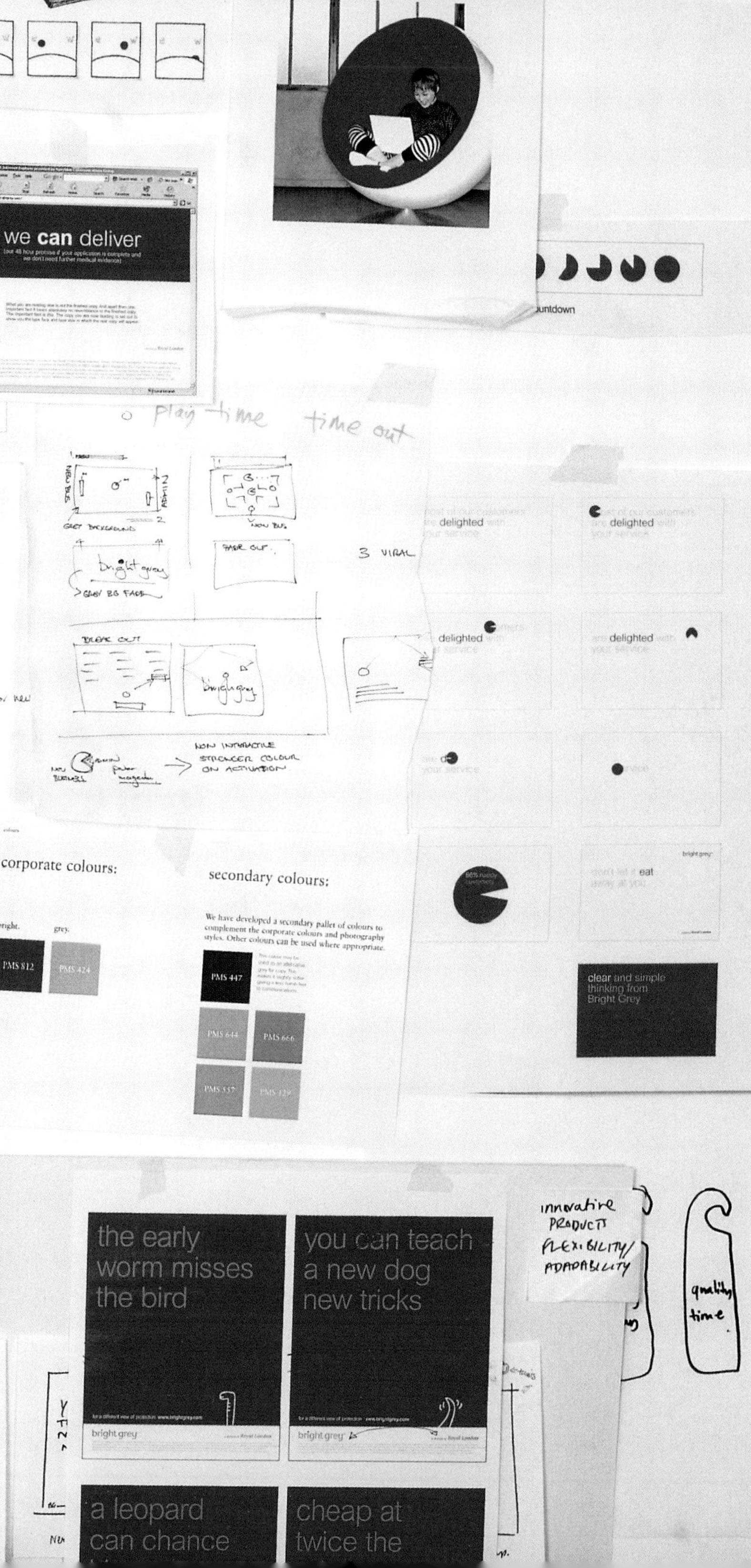

Financial services deregulation, new methods of product delivery and the end of traditional retail hierarchies and separations, mean that a supermarket can sell everything from banking to books to baking and bank branches close to become restaurants and bars and their services go on-screen or online. For new products, more opportunity means more competition, so more care in marketing and naming.

Royal London Insurance asked Navyblue for help with a new individual "lifestyle protection" insurance package. To make the name work, Navyblue focussed not on the market but on what the product did – it helped with the difficult areas of life, such as illness and redundancy. Bright Grey was the result: lightening up the grey areas of life (and your grey matter is bright if you protect yourself, as well). "We have gained a huge amount of experience from creating the Bright Grey look, feel and tone of voice and research has shown how important these elements are", John Smart reports. The result is that the product stands out from the diffuse mass of the competition, even if the visual token of this is only a magenta dot.

112

EC1 DEPT
H5336 C
005 LEEM

"Dogs", W.H. Auden assured us, "go on with their doggy life". Without pausing for the camera, as Navyblue found when trying to shoot one of five images for the Boots gift cards commissioned in 2002. But the real challenge was not the posing pet but the mechanics of the card and its mount. The concept was for the customer to take card and mount to the checkout, where the required sum could be credited to the magnetic strip on the card. The plastic card could then be folded into the cardboard holder (on which a message could be written) to make a gift pack. Which in turn could be tagged onto another gift. Oh and the item was displayed in-store either standing in a box or slung from a hanger. And once the paper mechanics were solved, the designs on the cards and their mounts had to apply to a range of closely grouped niche markets. And be for all occasions, even though they were launched at Christmas. Incidently the dog photographed (as shown) was not selected for the final design. Who says it's a dog's life?

110

Boots
Giftcard
for someone special...
Giftcard
for someone special...
Boots

108

Photography: Robbie Smith Tel: +44 131 556 0345

when we won't pay a claim
bright grey
Key Features of the Bright Grey Protection Plan
(November 2003)
This document contains important information
about your Bright Grey Protection Plan and
the covers you can choose. You should read
this along with your quote.
Our commitment
Risk factors
Its aims
Your commitment
a division of Royal London

Photography: Nisbet & Wylie Tel: +44 141 226 3888

Richie, Senior Designer

Hotels are only superficially places, in a sense. What often makes a visit to a hotel memorable is the people, not the things: the friendly concierge or the pleasant barman, rather than the furniture or the finishes. So in creating an annual report for the Hilton Group, Navyblue needed to balance the immediate perception of the group as a hotel group, with the fact that its other interests including Ladbrokes, Vernons Pools, LivingWell, Scandic and Conrad were equally important and sometimes more profitable. The team sought not only to stress the diversity of the people working for the group around the world, but also to emphasise the human element that is the common thread of the group's overall business. Each staff member's individual story is part of the shared goal of caring for customers: the breadth of the group is expressed by those who represent it.

Navyblue's involvement with Miller Homes began with an annual report, moved on into identity work and most recently into a successful website (research shows that one in five buyers of a new Miller home had previously registered on the Miller website). This is what the work spells out. But look behind the work and what is happening is somewhat subtler. Miller, a successful housebuilder in the Scottish market, has moved both into a wider market and into a new role, as a creator of communities.

This is in part a change of scale but more importantly a change of self-perception. Here Navyblue played an important role, in developing an identity that was not only a visual expression of the company but empowered a new definition of the company's role and purpose.

Photography: Stewart & Baxter Tel: +44 131 659 6262

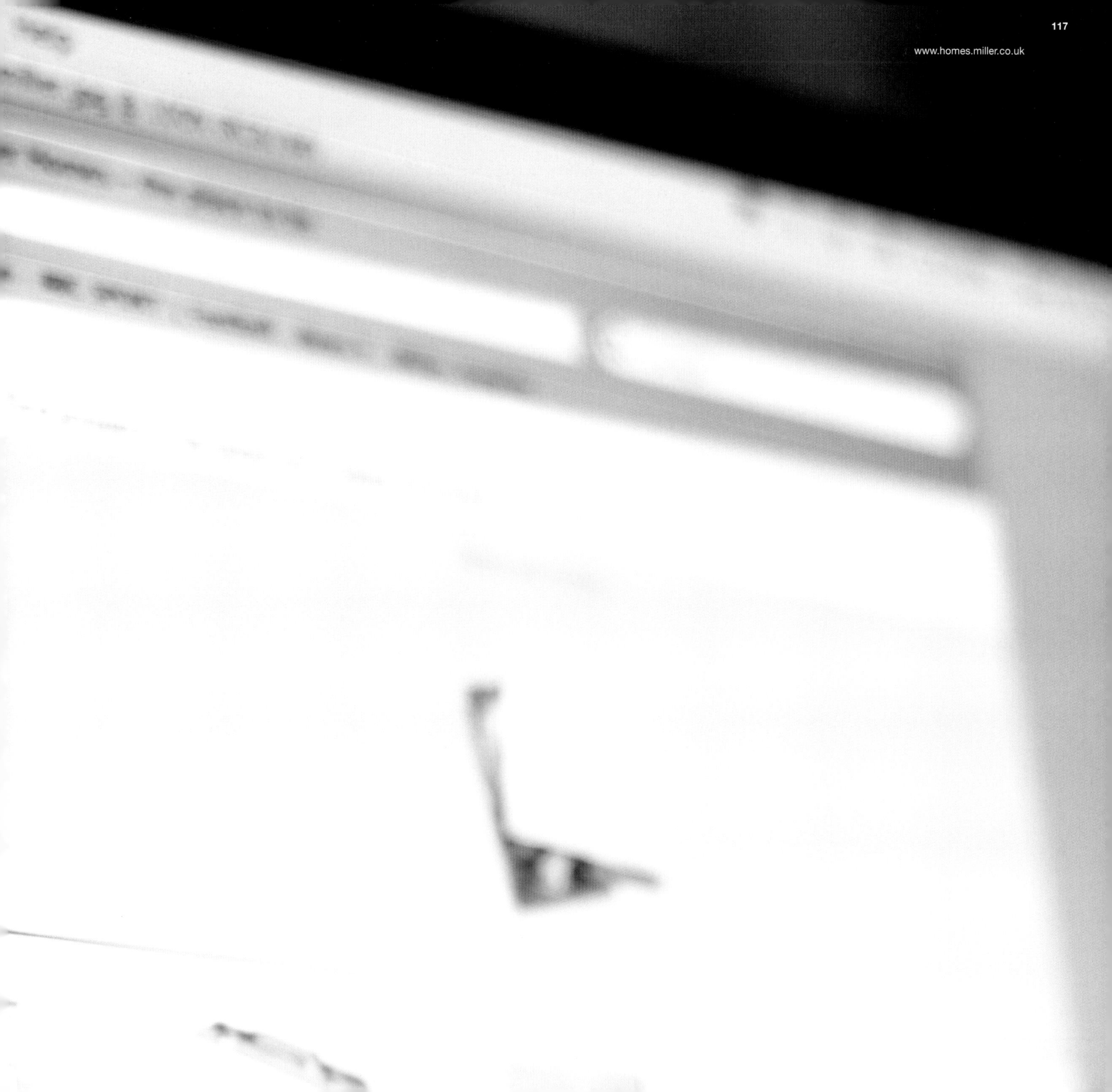

"Oh no! I have to touch up a pie"

Jonathan, Creative Artworker

Photography: Douglas Jones Tel: +44 131 557 2200

Make sure
food is fully

Photography: David N McIntyre Tel: +44 07977574151

Chairman's statements, auditor's reports, profit and loss accounts, balance sheets: the formal contents of annual reports are clearly fixed and for very good reasons of fairness and probity. But at the same time what shareholders and other parties really want from an annual report is to get a feel for the company and that doesn't necessarily fit on a simple A4 page. The choice of image, typography and presentation of a report can convey the context a company operates in and its values, whether shouted on street corners like the vendors of the Trinity Mirror group's newspapers, or passed around quietly, as with the carefully balanced advice offered by the Scottish Tourist Board. In each case the designer's task was to find the appropriate visual vehicle.

122

TRINITY MIRROR plc, Sunday, 30th December 2001

EXTRA EXTRA

a year

Retailing is getting more international, both in that retailers are sourcing goods worldwide, and that established brands have a global reach. One brand doing both is Body Shop, retailing natural cosmetics and associated products around the world. Their gift boxes had to work across all markets, and Navyblue were asked to help make this happen. The designers turned to the regions and cultures the goods came from, building up pattern and colour vocabularies for different areas – Africa, South America, India and so on. These ranges of colours, patterns and images of celebration provided motifs to be used on the bands of the gift boxes, which in turn could contain products from the featured areas, or be related to a specific part of the body. The concept created themes for the products: it was about branding rather than packaging.

Photography: Euan Myles Tel: +44 131 659 5445

Photography: Iain Stewart Tel: +44 131 453 4138

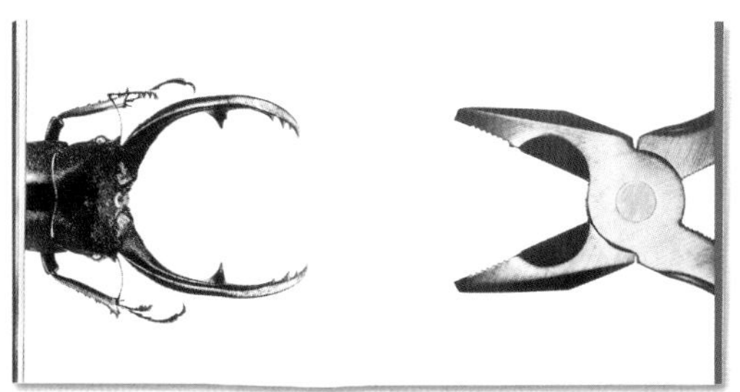

fridge magnets
keep
Prepare and store raw
raw meat
keep pets away from food dishes and worktops
TURN
front door illuminates
keep hot food hot
cooker.
check
use-by dates
bug
magnifying glasr
Keep surfaces clean
shopping bag
Put chilled and frozen food in your fridge or freezer as soon as you can.

The trade fair and the funfair at one time shared the same space, the marketplace, where in the centre of village or town business and enjoyment went together. Navyblue remembered this when asked by the Food Standards Agency to create a stand reminding the public about safe means for preparing food, as part of Foodfest in Glasgow. Surprise and wit can get a message home as effectively – perhaps more effectively – than sober preaching, so the designers created a comically exaggerated 3-D cartoon kitchen as a stage for delivering the food safety message.

Marie Langton, Glanbia
Group Communications Manager

the scooby snack

ingredients

11 slices of white bread
60 ml (4 tbsp) mayonnaise
8 large sliced beef tomatoes
600g (21oz) wafer thin honey roast ham
1 sliced Iceberg lettuce
10 slices cheddar cheese
Sea salt and black pepper for seasoning
Preparation time: 15 minutes

how to make it

1 Take the first slice of premium white bread, spread a little mayonnaise – add 4 slices of beef tomato – 25g of wafer thin honey roast ham, a covering of Iceberg lettuce and top with a processed cheese slice

2 Add a little sea salt and pepper for seasoning and then place a second slice of bread on top – repeat again until you have a tower. If you are transporting the snack – use a metal kebab skewer to secure

3 Ideal served on its own (which should be quite enough) or with French Fries spread around the base of the snack

Serves: 1 with a large appetite

Photography: Shannon Tofts Tel: +44 131 554 2154

Many a good design, it has been said, started as a scribble on a piece of paper. The truth is that many scribbles on many pieces of paper are what produces the final answer, as the initial concept is refined, tuned and shaped to an exact understanding of the brief, an exercise balancing gesture and control. Such was the case for the new identity for Newcastle International Airport. Once the graphic mark had been defined, the task was to integrate it into an identity system and roll out the new arrangement across the airport. This is a context where signage and wayfinding have a particular importance and the attention to detail needed to create a successful result from the original concept is echoed in the development of the final result on site.

Can you spot the difference as the design progresses...

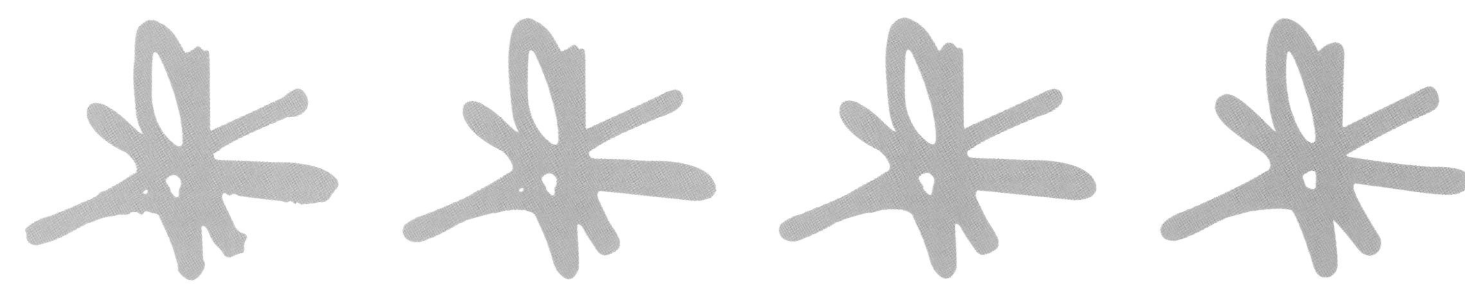

134

Newcas
AIRPORT TAXIS
NA52 AAU

International

← Holiday Flights
→ Domestic Arrivals

132

Photography: Stewart & Baxter Tel: +44 131 659 6262

ime
o plump
p the
ushions

closing

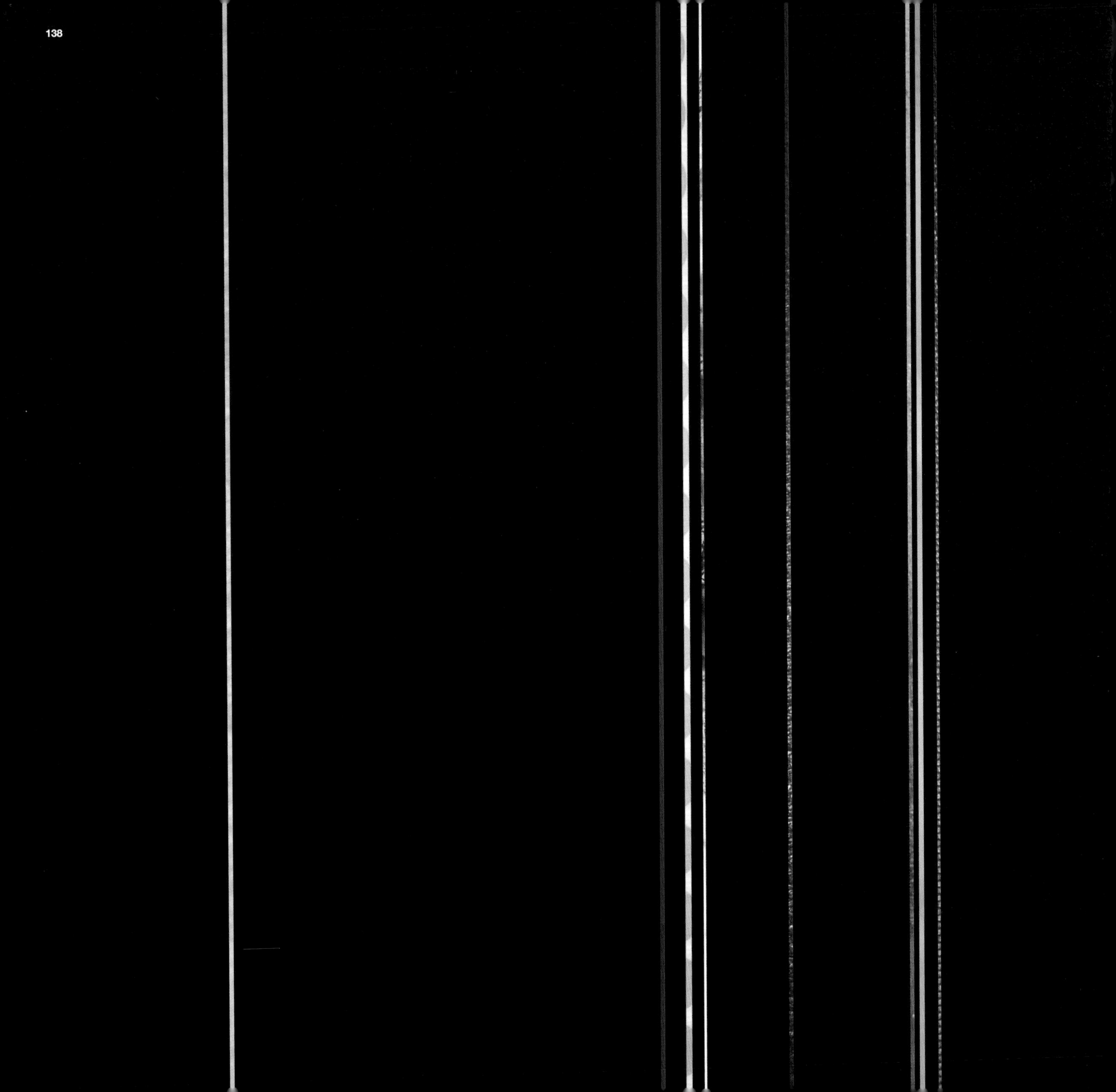

let's show you some more...

Putting together a portfolio seems at first like a visual exercise: placing each item so that it is in balance with the others, so that its qualities are not swamped by its neighbours, but also so that the whole overall effect gets the right message across. Which would be fine if the items involved were finite, as it were, but they are not. Each image – as on the following pages – is both finished and unfinished, complete and incomplete. Finished and complete in the sense that it is the piece of work – poster or book or website or fair stand or advert or identity – that was approved by client and designer and seen by the public, but unfinished in that so often each individual item is just one marker on a longer journey designer and client are taking together, and incomplete in that behind the finished item there is a narrative, an exchange, a relationship, and the item is part of that history too.

So putting together a portfolio is also an exercise in memory, and an emotional judgement as well as an aesthetic one. And putting it together is important, as a way of reviewing what one has done, as a way of refreshing one's ideas, and – perhaps most importantly – as a way of thanking all those clients whose challenges and whose encouragements brought all the work into being.

36% increase in profit before tax
19% increase in operating profit
14% increase in turnover
15% increase in dividend

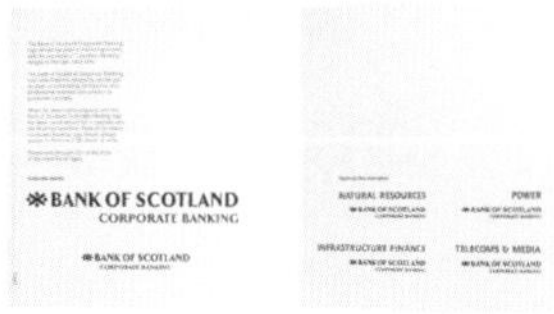

2
BODY
SOUL
O

bright grey™

a big challenge

ng²

a year on

bright grey

on

on budget

time to plump up the cushions

38,000

1billion

handbags and gladrags

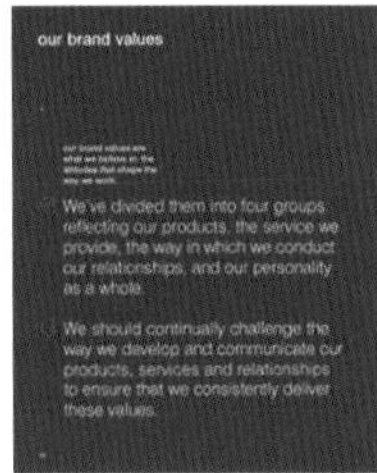

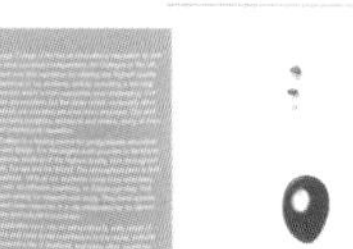

eca
edinburgh college of art

Doing business...

"Running a ports business is not just about ships, it's about service. And it's not just about handling cargo, it's about adding value."

Syrah

Chardonnay

Merlot

Sauvignon Blanc

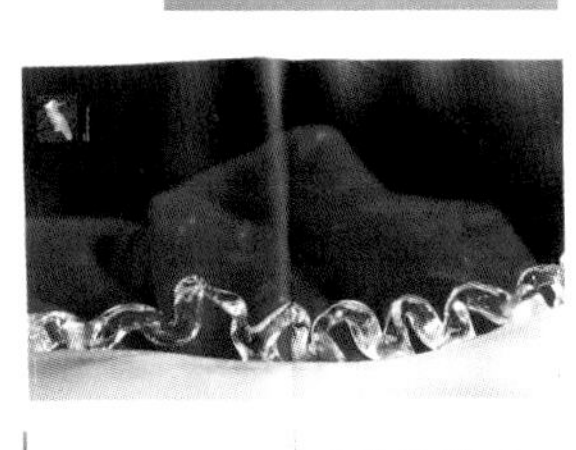

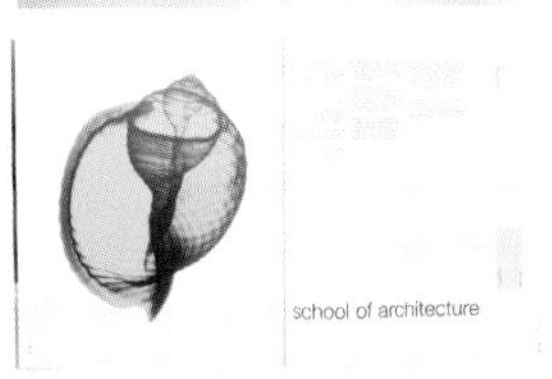

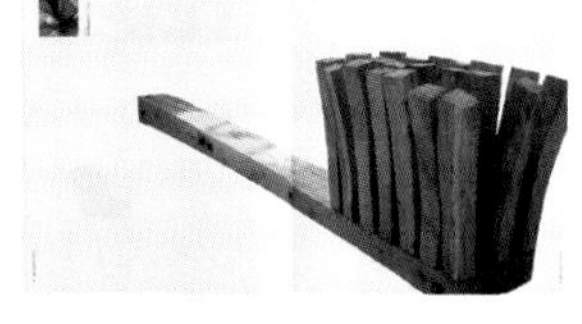

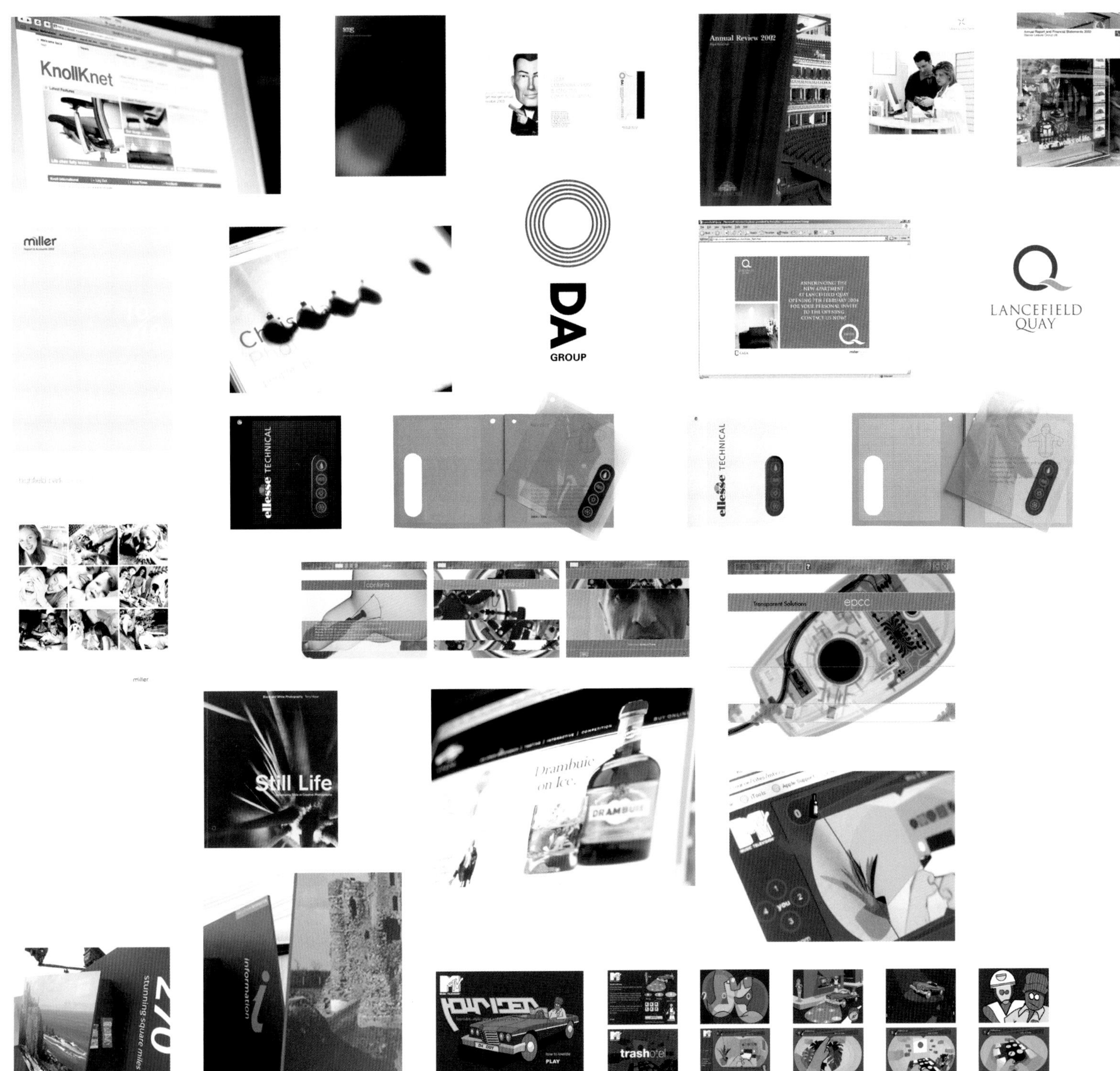
KnollKnet
Annual Review 2002
DA
GROUP
miller
LANCEFIELD
QUAY
ANNOUNCING THE
NEW APARTMENT
AT LANCEFIELD QUAY
OPENING 7TH FEBRUARY 2004
FOR YOUR PERSONAL INVITE
TO THE OPENING
CONTACT US NOW!
ellesse TECHNICAL
ellesse TECHNICAL
contents
epcc
Transparent Solutions
miller
Still Life
Drambuie
on Ice.
DRAMBUIE
stunning square miles
information
trashotel
PLAY

Chris Hall
Photography
people places studio

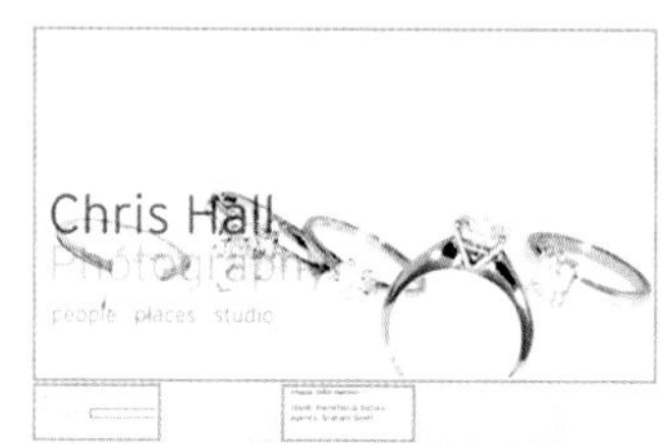
Chris Hall
people places studio

Chris Ha
people places studio

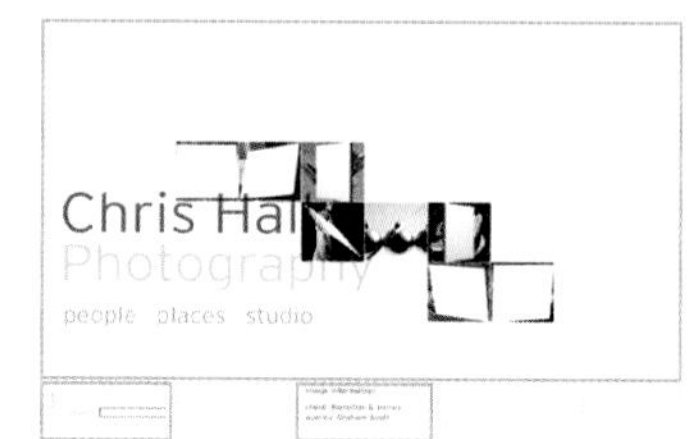
Chris Hal
people places studio

MORE PEOPLE

Baxters
FRESH SOUP
Mediterranean
Tomato

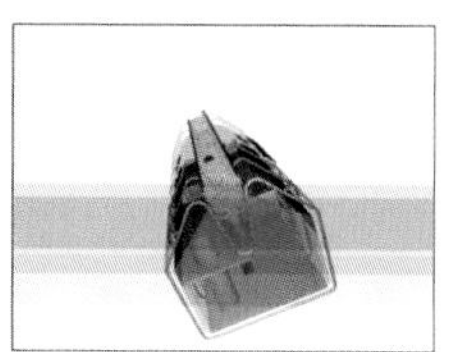

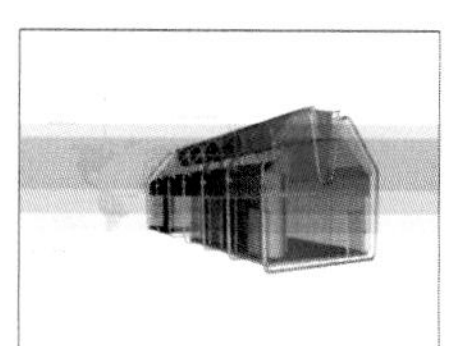

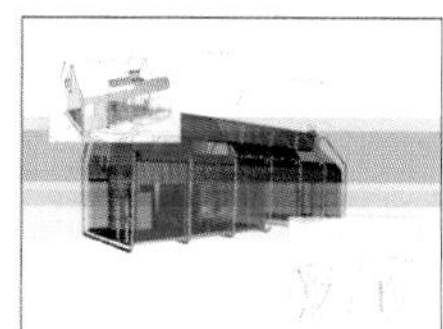

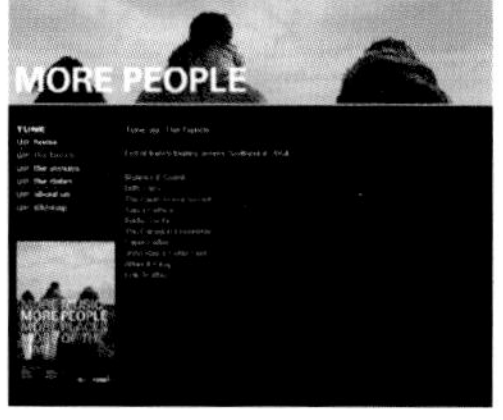
MORE PEOPLE

Geest
talks

Talking
numbers

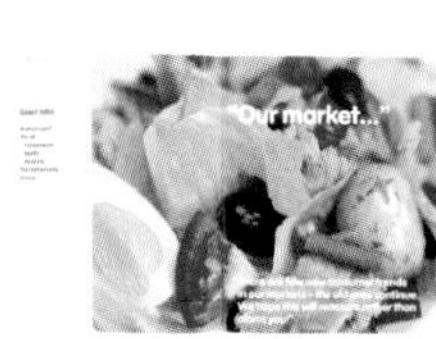
"Our market..."

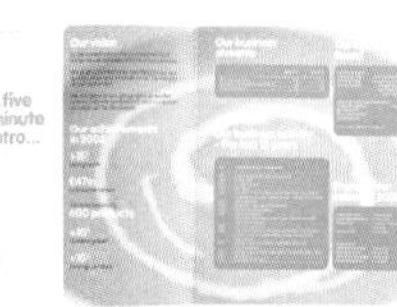
"A five
minute
intro..."

MORE MUSIC

ellesse

ellesse

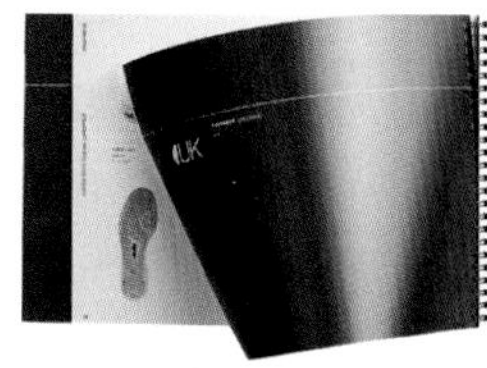

ellesse
ellesse

ellesse
ellesse

ellesse

SHAKERMAKER

AMSTERDAM

SHAKERMAKER

miller

UKFILM

newbold green
the place that's going to be the place to be
2, 3 and 4 bedroomed homes
miller homes

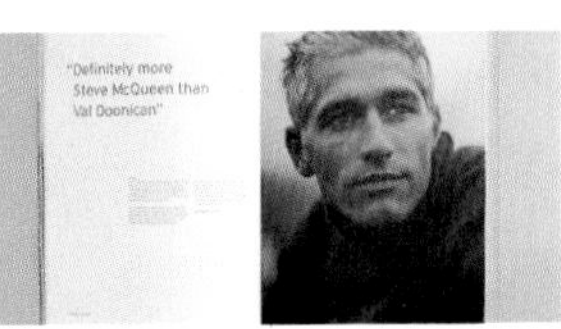
"Definitely more Steve McQueen than Val Doonican"

MORE MUSIC
MORE PEOPLE
MORE PLACES
MORE OF THE TIME
TUNED

MORE MUSIC
MORE PEOPLE
MORE PLACES
MORE OF THE TIME
TUNED

MORE MUSIC
MORE PEOPLE
MORE PLACES
MORE OF THE TIME
TUNED

MORE MUSIC
MORE PEOPLE
MORE PLACES
MORE OF THE TIME
TUNED

ellesse

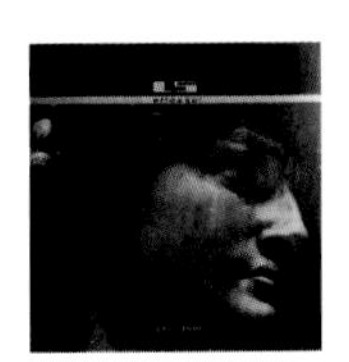

Brand Values
Dixons Group plc
Thank you for shopping

get inside

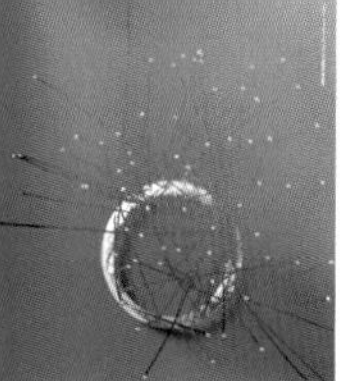

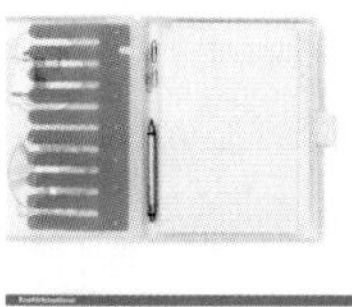

Newcastle International

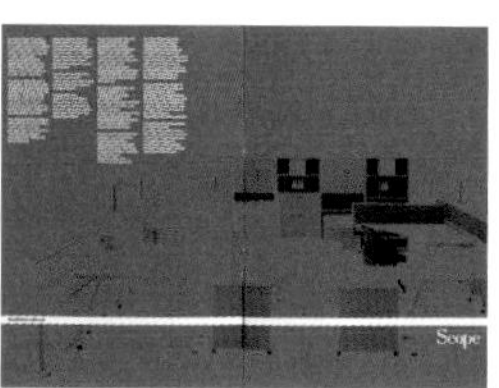

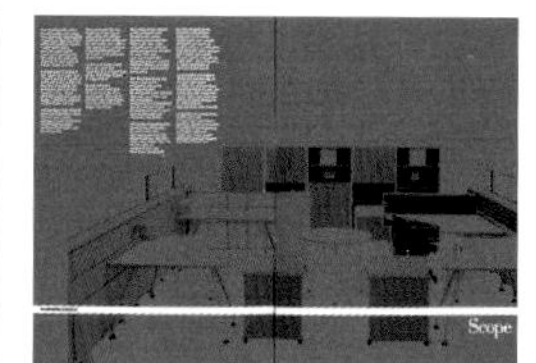

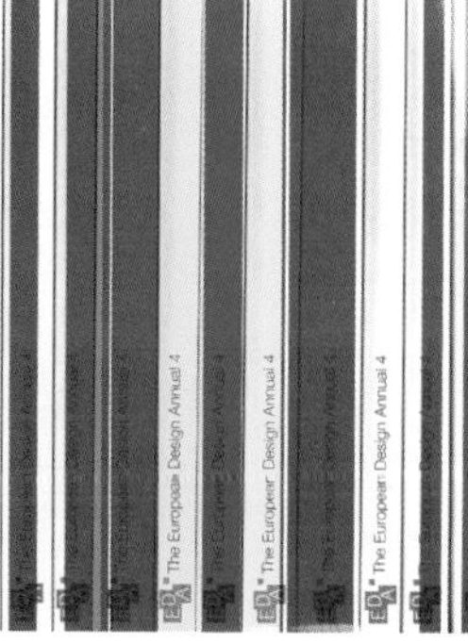

miller

Baxters
FRESH SOUP
Chicken Broth

Baxters
FRESH SOUP
Garden Pea and Mint

Baxters
FRESH SOUP
Carrot and Coriander
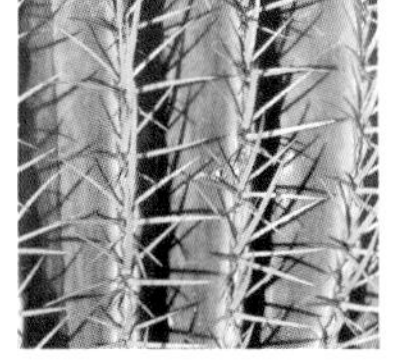

Baxters
FRESH SOUP
Classic Minestrone

Baxters
FRESH SOUP
Country Mushroom

Baxters
FRESH SOUP
Thai Chicken Noodle

bond

"/Robert Horne's 2001 'calendar' this year has a new and exciting twist to it. Working with partners navyblue and Fulmar Colour, Robert Horne has produced a highly visual and tactile Yearbook. Designed around the needs of blind and partially sighted people, this amazing production combines print, paper and design with beautiful imagery based upon the sensual world of texture, form and colour within a garden.

Baxters
FRESH SOUP
Classic French Onion

Baxters
FRESH SOUP
Creamy Broccoli and Stilton

Baxters
FRESH SOUP
Traditional Scotch Broth

Baxters
FRESH SOUP
Chunky Winter Vegetable

Baxters
FRESH SOUP
Borscht

Baxters
FRESH SOUP
Chicken Gumbo
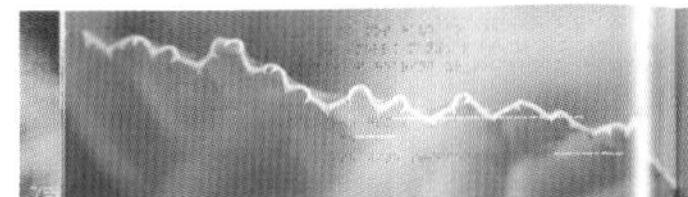

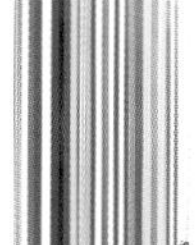

Profitez-en:
Montrez-vous
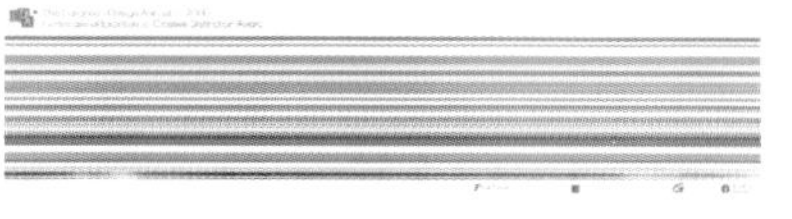
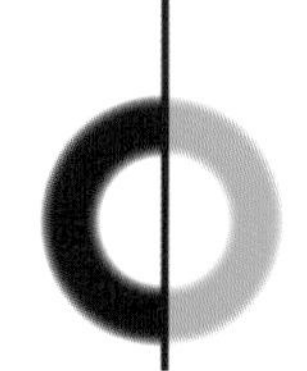

dancebase

Drambuie on Ice.
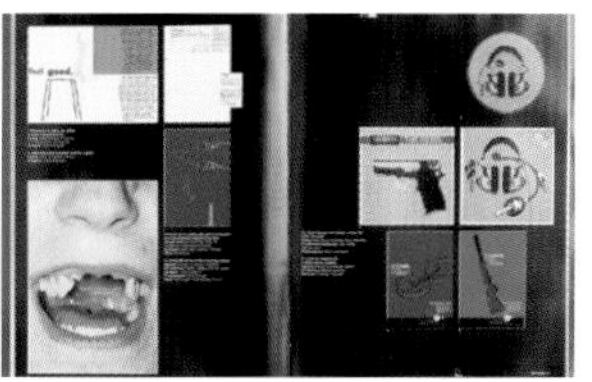

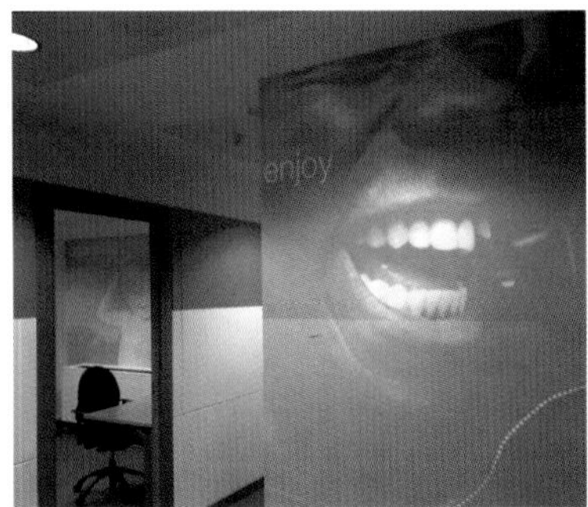
enjoy

cushty
gossip

you're great

chill

Russel+Aitken

Enduring evolving

Founded on principle
inspired by innovation

A single source
through every channel

Portraits
Nudes

Landscapes

Black and White
Photography

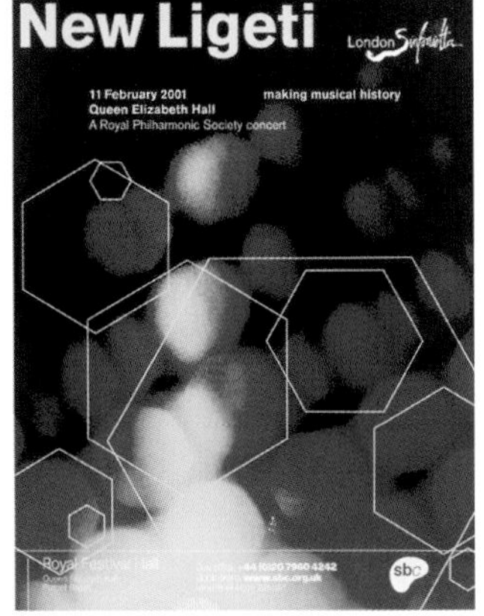
New Ligeti
11 February 2001
Queen Elizabeth Hall
making musical history
A Royal Philharmonic Society concert

From the desert to the lakes
Birtwistle

Vivico
REAL ESTATE

Season 1999/2000
Music of the bizarre
Routes from Stravinsky

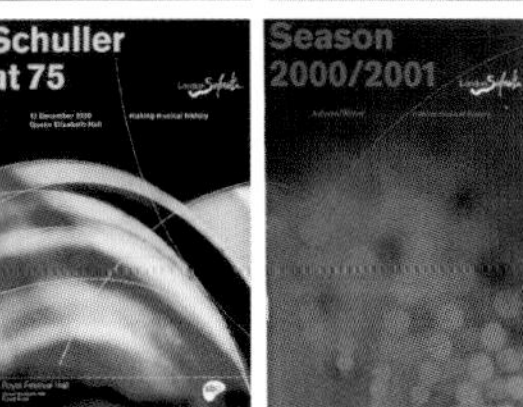
Schuller at 75
Season 2000/2001

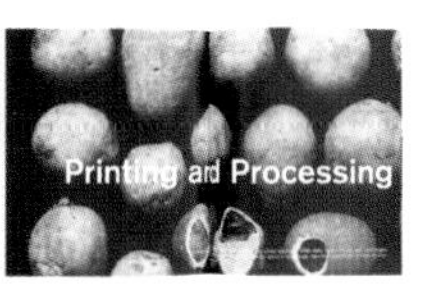
Printing and Processing

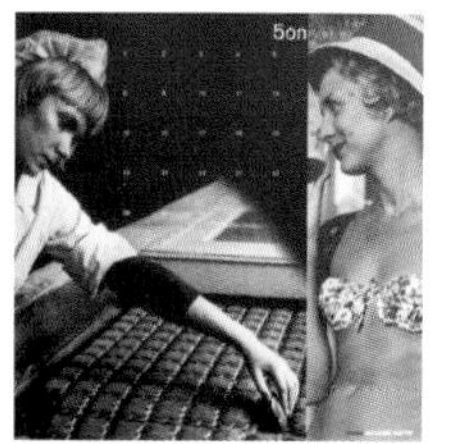

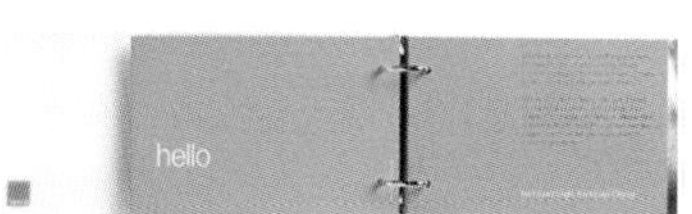

BOROUGH

thebathroom

100% Design
1e Europe
A G Barr
Adventi
AGOY
Ahlstrorm
Alba Centre
Alliance Unichem
Almeida Theatre
Amec
Amersham
Ancestral Scotland
Artisan
Assembly Direct
Associated British Ports
Axiis
Ayrshire BTC
Badenoch and Clark
Baillie Gifford
Balfour Beatty Construction
Ballantyne
Bank of Scotland
Barnsley Theatre Trust
Barrie Cashmere
Barrington Stoke
Bass Brewers
Baxters of Speyside
Beattie Media
BDC Events
Black & White Publishing
Blacks Leisure Group
Bluecycle.com
Bond Advertising
Boots
Borderline Theatre
Boredom Free Zone
Brandon Motors
Bright Grey
British Steel Pensions
British Tourist Authority
Brunswick Group
Brush Factory
BT Scotland
Buck UK
Burrell Company
Business Design Centre
Business For Sterling
Business in the Community
Cairn Energy
Calmont
Carnegie Hall
Carrick Jewellery
Carrick Neil
CAT Technologies
Catchline Public Relations
CB Hillier Parker
Chelsea Crafts Quarter
CIGNA
CIS
Citigate
City of Edinburgh Council
Clark Scott-Harden
Clear Representations
Clydeport
Collins Debden
Colourlink Creative Imaging
Commissum
Communicado Theatre Company
Company Growth Team
Conran & Partners
Corus Packaging Plus
Countryside Residential
Countrywide Porter Novelli
Coverdale Davis Communications
Crafts Council
Crown Office
CSCT
DA Group
Dance Base
Datalink Computers
Dawson Cashmere Company
Dawson International
Dazzle
DEGW
Delphic Group
Derwent Valley Development
Design Council
Design Museum
Digitlink
Dixons Group
DM Panetta
dmgAngex
DMS Scotland
Donaldsons
Drambuie Liqueur Company
Drummond Miller
DTZ
Dundee High School
Dunedin Capital Partners
Dunedin Independent
Dunedin Systems
East London Business Alliance
East Lothian Council
East Scot. European P'ship
Eclipse Blinds
ELTB
Edinburgh Chamber of Commerce
Edinburgh C C Mgmt
Edinburgh College of Art
Edinburgh Film Festival
Edinburgh Film Focus
Edinburgh First
Edinburgh Folk Festival
Edinburgh Fund Managers
Edin. Intl. Film Festival
Edinburgh Rugby
Edinburgh Sitters
Eglinton
EICC
Elbow Room
Ellesse
Engineering Council
English National Opera
Enterprise Alliance
Enterprise Ayrshire
Enterprise Services Scotland
EPCC
Ethicon
Euro 2008 Bid
European Design Annual
Event Scotland
Ewart Consultancy Associates
Excel
Excell Biotech
Eyestorm
Farrel Furniture
Federation of Scottish Theatre
Fender Sturrock

Fibernet
Fife College
Fife Enterprise
Filmhouse
Fiona Scott Communications
FM Developments
Food Standards Agency
Football Association of Ireland
Forest Enterprise
Forestry Commission
Foundation for Sport and the Arts
Fox Kids Europe
Frankfurt EDA
Fulham Football Club
Future Focus
Garden History Society
Garden Stonecraft
GB Telecom
GC Investments
Geest
Georgeson Office Interiors
GF Smith
Gifford Stewart & Co
Glanbia
Glgw Col Nautical Studies
Glasgow Development Agency
Glasgow Film Theatre
Glasgow Rugby
Glasgow Tourism Training Unit
Glenmorangie
Global Farmers
Gordon & MacPhail
Grampian Enterprise
Grampian Hospitality
Grayston Alan & Durtnell
Great Circle Communications
Great Scottish & Western Railway
Greenwood Clothing
Groovy Chocolate.com
Guardian Employee Benefits
Gyle Shopping Centre
Hammerson UK Properties
Haslemere
HBoS Group
HEBS
Henderson Boyd Jackson
Hermitage Investments
High School of Dundee
Hi-Tec Sports
Highland Spring
Highland Strategic Holdings
Highland Village Taverns
Highlands & Islands Enterprise
Hilton Group
Hoggs of Fife
Ian Macleod
Ian McLaughlin Associates
Ideal Standard
In Video
Incisus
IndigoVision Group
Infratech
Ink Tank
Innes & Grieve
Inside Right
Inside Space
Insideout
Intelligent Finance
Intermusica
International Design Fair
International Tartans
Invergordon Distillery
IP Premium Papers (Zanders)
Iridium Arts
ISM Solutions
ITouch
IVP
Jack Morton Worldwide
Jackel International
Java Investment Trust
Jewel & Esk Valley College
Jim Anderson
Jim Beam Brands
Jockey UK
John Wood Group
Johnstone Media
Joint Nature Conservation
Jones Lang Lasalle
JP Morgan
KAL
Kensingtons
Kilgraston School
Kilmartin Property
King Sturge & Co
Kingdom of Fife Tourist Board
Knoll International
Lambey Gilchrist Consultancy
Lastminute.com
Lauder College
Laurent Perrier
Learning & Skills Council
Learning & Teaching - Scotland
LEEL
Leith Development Company
Lexmark International Scotland
Lloyds TSB Scotland
Local Gov. Information Bureau
Loft Living (Medway)
Lomond Shores Management
London 2012
London Sinfonietta
Lothian Electric Machines
Lothian Regional Council
Lothian TAP Agency
Luke Hughes
Lyon Windram Crolla
Macdonald Hotels
Mackenzie River Travel
MacRoberts Arts Centre
Maksu Group of Hotels
Marketing Mechanics
Marketing Zone
Mary Erskine Junior School
Maximillion
McLaurin Communications
Menzies Group
Merchant Corporate Design
Micromode Medical
Midlothian Council
Milknosugar
Miller Civil Engineering
Miller Construction
Miller Developments
Miller Group
Miller Homes
Miller Mining
Milo Cosmetics
MoDo Merchants
Modus
Morag Ballantyne
Motorola
MTV
Napier University
National Museums of Scotland
New Europe
New Land Assets
Newcastle Breweries
Newcastle International Airport
NHS Health Scotland
Nimmos Colour Printers
Oasis Stores
Obvious Solutions
Ocean Terminal Shopping Centre
Office Systems Scotland
One Swoop.com
Orange
Origin Australia
Origin Information Technology
Origin UK
Oxford Orchestra da Camera
Paisley Arts Centre
Pennant
Performance Direct
Perth & Kinross Council
Perth Festival of the Arts
Perth TCM
Peter J Gadsby
Petrasco Services
Photonica
Pilscher Hershmann
Powles Hunt & Sons
PR Executive
PR Promotions
Pringle of Scotland
Prior Communications
Pulse Group
QBiogene
Quality Meat Scotland
Quantum Glass
Quilvest
Rangers Football Club
Realise
Red Events
Reebok International
REHIS
Renfrewshire Enterprise
Richard Corsie Leisure
Richmond Towers
Ridgemont UK
Riverford Mill
RiversGani Communications
Robert Horne Group
Rolls-Royce
Roofline
Ross PR
Rotovision
Royal Bank of Scotland
RIAS
Royal Mail National
RSAMD
RTM
Russel & Aitken
Russell Europe
Ryden International
S B Englands
Safeguard Continuity
Sanderson Young Estate Agents
Sanmex
Scotmat
Scotsman Publications
Scotsman.com
Scottish & Newcastle
Scottish Arts Council
Scottish Bobath Association
Scottish Brewers
Scottish Convention Bureau
Scot. Council Single Homeless
Scottish Courage Brewing
Scottish Courage Exclusive Brands
Scottish Enterprise
Scottish Equitable
Scottish Equity Partners
Scottish Executive
Scottish Film Council
Scottish Fine Soaps
Scottish Football Association
Scot. Higher Ed. Funding
Scottish Homes
Scottish International
Scottish Legal Aid Board
Scottish Life
Scottish Media Group
Scottish Museums Council
Scottish Mutual
Scottish Natural Heritage
Scottish Portrait Gallery
Scottish Provident
Scottish Rugby Union
Scottish Screen
Scottish Seabird Centre
Scottish Widows
Seafish Industry Authority
Search Recruitment & Selection
Send Group
Shandwick Scotland
Shell International
Shilland & Co
Signum Industries
Simkins Partnership
Sixty Watt
Slater Hogg Howison
Soleco UK
South Eastern Museum Service
Sport Scotland
Springfords
SSK
St Andrew's Bay Hotel and Resort
St Andrews University
St Edmunds Hall College
St Giles Cathedral
St Leonards & St Katherines Sch
Standard Life
Stannifer Developments
Stellar Quines Theatre Company
Stewart Milne Group
Stocktrade
Strathcastel
Syquest Technologies
TAG Theatre Company
Take Control
Taylor & Fraser
Tektra
Telford College
Telstar Video Entertainment
The Alliance Partnership
The Body Shop
The Borough Hotel
The British Council
The Communication Group
The EDI Group
The Executive Centre
The Factory Residents Association
The Federation of Scottish Theatre
The Glasgow Alliance
The Lighthouse
The List
The Lord Roberts Workshop
The Marketing Store Worldwide
The Nowell Partnership
The Phonebox
The Royal Albert Hall
The Royal Scotsman
The Royal Society
The Stationery Office
The Witchery by the Castle
THUS
Todd & Duncan
Tods Murray WS
Tony Stone Images
Tony Walker Interiors
Topps Tiles
Tourism Training Executive
Tower Restaurant
Traveline
Traverse Theatre
Tree Tops Development Co
Trinity Mirror
Trylogy
Tuckwell Press
Turnbull Jeffrey Partnership
UK Film Council
UK Trade & Investment
Unite Group
United Distillers
University of Aberdeen
University of Edinburgh
University of Glasgow
University of St Andrews
University of Strathclyde
Urban Renaissance
USC Group
Valente McCombie Hunter
Valuations Office Agency
Vida
Virgin Group
Virgin Publishing
Visit Scotland
Vyson
Wallis Hunter
Water Industry Commissioner
Watermark Landscaping
Waterside Television
Waverley Vintners
Webscotland
Wheeler
Willoughby Public Relations
Wilson Bowden Development
Wood Group
Wood4
Xpert Solutions
Yo-tel
Zig Zag Designer Knitwear

where next?

58

"I'd been a director of a couple of other agencies before starting Navyblue", Doug Alexander points out, "and I'd often been promised an eventual equity share but nothing ever happened. We did not want that to be the case with Navyblue. Thus, in the usual Navyblue 'let's give it a go and see what happens' manner, we have looked at different options over the years to provide a long-term structure, as a way to secure the future and extend our activity".

So Navyblue has a new board of directors, creating opportunities for a second generation of designers to lead the company in due course. And generation is the appropriate word, in that several of the new directors have also recently become parents, a coincidence Geoff Nicol finds "curious but satisfying". Look around the offices and infants beam from many a screensaver. In ten years, Navyblue has moved from being a vibrant, young design agency to being a vibrant, young design agency: or rather, design group.

Their skills base has deepened, their client list has grown stronger, they operate out of two locations (and are thinking of a third, if they find the right partners), they have added three-dimensional and web design and strategic consultancy to the offer (and are starting on advertising) but the vigour, drive and sense of opportunity are still there, stronger, even, through experience. It is not even stamina: more that it is a vortex of energy that is continually generated from the contact with colleagues and clients and through a shared vision of the potential of the group.

A major potential client once asked a Navyblue presentation team if they liked football. He received the next morning an audio cassette celebrating Barnsley's FC's recent promotion entitled, "It's just like watching Brazil". The measure of aptness and insouciance in the response stands for the directness and passion Navyblue bring to everything they do.

Justin, Senior Designer
rum cocktail

ingredients

2 1½ oz. light rum
1 lime
1 tbsp simple syrup
Mint leaves (8 or so sprigs worth)
Ice
Club soda
Tall glass
Spoon, or some other utensil that can be used to mash the mint leaves

how to make it

1 Make simple syrup: Heat equal parts sugar and water in a saucepan until just before boiling and stir until the sugar has completely dissolved

2 Place the mint leaves and 1 tbsp of the simple syrup (cooled) in the glass, then squish it all around with a spoon (or whatever appropriate utensil you can find) for 20-30 seconds, until you can smell that good minty smell

3 Cut the lime in half, getting rid of the seeds as well as you can. Squeeze the juice out from both halves into the glass, then throw one half into the glass

4 Pour in the rum and stir

5 Add plenty of ice, then top off the mixture with club soda. Garnish with a sprig of mint and drink

6 Repeat 1-5 several times

Photography: Shannon Tofts Tel: +44 131 554 2154

I think we all deserve a drink now...

cheers

Why did you want to work for Navyblue

Doug - It was always my ambition to set up my own design group and I am always glad we did.

Karl - The money.

Pete - Seemed like a nice bunch of like-minded people.

Geoff - We set up Navyblue to operate on our own terms, to make our mark (in terms of success) and to try and make an impact in the world of design.

Natalie M - After being interviewed for the 1st time - (1st time round...) it has been a long haul for me... 3 years in fact before I secured a job with Navyblue... I actually was interviewed by 5 different people. Anyway, having walked though the door for the 1st time, my gut reaction was "I could work there... I want to work there... I will work there!"

Mike L - At the time they were new, had a good reputation and I was warned to stay away from them, which naturally attracted me.

Caroline T - I was asked and was delighted to get back to doing some marketing and with Navyblue.

Toby - All kinds of reasons. Mike interviewed me and I really wanted to work with him. I loved the environment (the studio that is, not Giles Street). I was bowled over by the portfolio and clients. I really wanted to be a part of the company and do what I could to help it move forward. I'm glad to say I've still got that desire.

Jon - Knew the directors well. I realised we had a lot in common. I appreciated what they had achieved in 4 years and I was confident that I could make a difference!

Clare - It was a new company that was at the beginning of its journey and provided an exciting opportunity to help shape a business through great work.

Colin - Always seen as the market leader wanting to explore new avenues in design and I thought I could help to add value to the company.

Richie - When I was young and foolish and I wanted to work in London, Navyblue had a strong reputation, ethos and having spent some time talking to Geoff I was convinced he was my type of boss and Navyblue was my kind of company. If things had been different I could have been emailing this from another desk in another capital city. When Suzanne and I decided it would be a positive life change to move away from the South of England, Edinburgh was a place on our short list of possible destinations, then the impression Geoff and Navyblue had made on me rekindled my interest - there were only three places I would have considered working, Navyblue made me an offer and I took the chance to make a career/life move - oh and Jon was from Yorkshire and liked footie.

Ian - Need for new challenge (how boring!)

Bernie - Because I was already working with Geoff and Doug at another agency and they asked me to join them. Too exciting an opportunity to miss and because we were already good mates - the work hard, play hard culture was already in full effect.

Helen - I desperately wanted to live in Edinburgh. I started coming for interviews here and realised the work in Edinburgh was great too. I came to Navyblue for a portfolio showing and met Jon. He was the first person I had showed my portfolio to where I felt completely relaxed, it was the personality and unpretentious nature of the people who worked here that sold Navyblue to me.

Jonathan H - I was looking for a new job within design while freelancing and had heard good reports about Navyblue.

Andy I - Had seen a lot of their work about and liked it. Looked like they had a lot of talented folk in their midst.

Dave - Creative agency with an interesting list of clients who where looking to improve their 3D offer.

Jen - The lively creative feel of the office when I was interviewed.

Nick - Jon and Doug persuaded me it was a good idea to leave my last company.

Bart - Right place, right time. Good work, good location - Clare and Geoff, my kinda people!

Justin - I ran out of money after drinking Pimms in Regents Park everyday for 2 months. So I needed a job. Navyblue is a design company. I'm a designer. I like their work. I think they like mine.

Mark - I like the typographic style and approach to design.

John D - The people (Pete and Toby) and the big blue wall.

Ray - It wasn't that I wanted to work for NB, it was that I wanted to work in the industry and they were the ones who took the gamble.

Malcolm - Young agency with a good reputation.

Caroline B - Good reputation - previous 'design consultancy of the year' and had won various other awards. Good timing - was leaving previous job at the same time that Navyblue was looking for someone!

Craig - Keeps me off the streets. As well as being a place where I have the opportunity to work at what I love doing. Its a chance to work with like-minded friendly people.

Natalie C - If this is where my career is at and I'm just starting out, who knows where it'll take me?

Rachel - A friend worked here and she always said I'd like it.

Jane - Hearing that Navyblue won the Scottish Equitable account.

Rosie - I kind of ended up here by default but I had heard lots about Navyblue previously and felt that it would be a positive move.

John S - I didn't really because I knew Bernie, Jon, Geoff and Doug and thought it would be weird to work with mates (seeing as they would be my bosses). I did a bit of freelance for a couple of weeks and then was heading back to New Zealand. What can I say, I'm still here!

Mike R - I wanted to work in a lively enthusiastic environment. I was really impressed by their approach to design and wanted to work within a good team.

Gavin - Passion!

Liza – A friend of mine who is a graphic designer recommended the company to me - said they pulled in a lot of high profile clients and had won quite a few awards over the years, so naturally I was intrigued.

Stuart - Because they are one of the top design consultancies in Britain.

Paul - I was asked.

Most memorable moment at Navyblue

Scott - Taking Scottish Equitable and Navyblue design team to focus groups and getting very positive feedback as to their value.

Karl - Getting a dart board and being office champ (The tourni is being played this evening, so I will confirm this on Monday!!) Update - Clare won!

Pete - Screaming in the car park after we won our first major pitch.

Doug - The last ten years.

Geoff - On the very first day of Navyblue, a client - Debbie O'Connor - turned up at the door with two bottles of champagne and a job! (I guess it was then I knew it was going to work). On a separate day in early 1995, another vision of loveliness turned up in the doorway of the breakfast hall of a B&B in Northumberland. Her name was Lizzie Cass - a photographic model we had arranged for a client's job later that day. To cut a long story short, I married her. Job done!

Natalie M - Eating the entire Malmaison Room Service Menu not once but twice between about 8 of us in world beating time of about 8½ minutes. A certain colleague doing a very, rather worryingly accurate impression of David Brent dancing!

Mike L - Probably winning our first Scottish Design Consultancy of the Year award in 1999. It was unexpected and we won 2 categories outright. I got a real buzz from that.

Caroline T - Meeting them for the first time in Maritime Lane, coming to work at Navyblue in Giles Street and seeing how the company has grown with so many talented and lovely people.

Toby - New ones are happening all the time - it's part of the reason I love this place! Some do stand out: Mike, a vacuum cleaner and a lift, Mike, a set of crutches and a Chinese restaurant. Jon getting through a huge jug of water during a presentation, then telling the client that the list of ingredients on a piece of packaging was "all in Foreign". Doug being described as an "agency overhead" in a client meeting. A very recent meeting in which the client described a colleague of his in a manner more colourful than I'm allowed to write. Nimmo's Golf Day 2002 - some great shots and some rather interesting bruising.

Jon - Satisfaction at building the creative team that we have. Winning any of the pitches. (In particular Euro 2008, Bright Grey and Newcastle Airport). Feeling that I had found my destiny. (I suppose the moment as a designer that you stop thinking about your own portfolio).

Clare - There have been many for good and bad reasons... but let's not talk about the bad! Probably getting made design director from a personal achievement perspective and otherwise it would probably be my first Navyblue Christmas party - the whole day!

Colin - There is not a particular moment that comes to mind but there always seems to be a buzz around the place and a very relaxed atmosphere.

Richie - Winning pitches for Scottish Screen, Hilton Group, Newcastle International, DA Group etc.

Ian - The euphoria surrounding us winning the Euro 2008 bid and the massive let down when we failed to host the event!

Bernie - The whole of the first year of Navyblue, although thinking about it, I don't remember a lot of it, it is just an emotional memory of feeling part of something special and having a direct effect on what was happening and being a master of my own destiny. My first pay rise from Geoff and Doug, following an approach from another company! My first board meeting – didn't have a clue! My first design award won for Navyblue (Gordon and MacPhail brochure) – very proud!

Helen - There are probably too many stories to even remember over the years but it's the people here and the laughs you have about anything and everything that make the moments memorable. Being made Senior Designer at Christmas.

Delia - My first Xmas night out with everyone (met the NB London staff - putting names to faces).

Jonathan H - Being offered the job.

Dave - The recent joint venture announcement.

Jen - Someone telling me I didn't 'look' Irish.

Nick - Bad - seriously over doing the sauce on our Christmas night out, Friday morning was, very very nasty. Good - nominated for young designer of the year and winning Navyblue's first ad account from an ad agency.

Bart - Receiving a top film buff book present even though my birthday was during Xmas period - dead chuffed!

Keith – Every day (and night) at Maritime Lane - such a laugh!

Ray - Yesterday.

Justin - Throwing Geoff's Atomic Kitten CD out of a 3rd floor window.

John D - Pete shouting "f**king yes" at the top of his voice in the carpark after winning the Ancestral Scotland pitch.

Malcolm – Yet to happen but ever hopeful!

Caroline B - I reckon I'm going to remember Paul's leaving night, for breaking my wrist.

Craig - The day I came to show my portfolio to Navyblue and left with a job! My mum was so proud.

Natalie C - Winning the Newcastle account.

Rachel - The day that my shower broke and I came into work with greasy hair, was asked if I minded getting my photo taken, as someone had dropped out. Just a 'black and white, back of the head shot' I was told, the 'colour, profile shot' has since appeared in a lot of Miller Homes brochures!

Rosie - Getting into a fight in the taxi queue at the Xmas party - whoops.

John S - Getting the news that we had won the SFA Euro 2008 job via text whilst lying on a beach in Vietnam on 23 December.

Liza - Has to be when Caroline fell and broke her wrist on the way to Paul's leaving do - girls and ice eh... dangerous combination.

Stuart - When Caroline came back from holiday with part of her finger cut off after having a little accident with a cigar cutter.

A story you would tell your best friend about Navyblue

Scott - Being responsible for the Euro 2004 creative. Internationally regarded as the best creative, just delivered poorly (not Navyblue's fault).

Karl - This one time, we all went for lunch and we forgot to order food - I suppose you had to be there.

Doug - There are so many and i'm certain there will be many more.

Geoff - There's a great story about chinese food, a meeting table and a receptionist but only good friends get to hear that one... There's a story about a trip to Germany but only really best friends get to hear that one.... Then there's the story of Doug Alexander setting fire to his face with a flamin' Sambucca at a Xmas party and I tell everyone that one (even taxi drivers). Navyblue is one long story. The memories knit together and shape the company as it is today. There's one for every occasion, sad, serious, saucy and so bloody funny.

Natalie M - I tell her lots of Navyblue stories... So much so, I think she wants to work here!

Mike L - Michael is the most common name for males in the English-speaking world. In over seven years at Navyblue there hasn't been another one in the company. Weird. In comparison, names like Ross, Christian/ Kristian and Holly are uncommon but there's been more than one of each of them!

Caroline T - Making the Navyblue CD experience.

Toby - It's a close run thing between Jon not being able to read "Foreign", and anything involving Mike.

Jon - In the pitch for 2008, the client asked what we felt about football. Doug sent the client a cassette entitled "Its just like watching Brazil" A celebration of Barnsley FC's promotion. It was a great response to the question and we went on to win the pitch!

There was the time I drank the entire jug of water whilst presenting after a very heavy night out. (This was even more memorable given the fact that I hadn't realised until Toby and Doug told me. Describing a proposal as "Damp" during the Bright Grey pitch much to Doug's amusement.

Clare - About the witching hour... this is when madness strikes between the hours of 12-3.00am and just about anything goes...

Twatbat, a game involving 2 players, an empty new studio, a brand new parque floor, wheelie chairs and customised bats made out of poster tubes with the most offensive name you can muster... (Leave that to your imagination). Scoring end to end goals-highest score wins (points knocked off for breakages).

Blind man bat, a similar game that involves any amount of players, an empty new studio, a brand new parque floor, wheelie chairs and customised bats made out of poster tubes with the most offensive name you can muster. One player is made blind with the help of an oversized woolly hat and then that player has to seek out the other players with his twatbat... The other players have to evade his detection by wheeling around the studio as quietly as they can so as not to give away their location!

Karaoke, I think we all know how this works except we use the radio to sing along to at full volume. Calling friends and family in the early hours to wake them up and generally laugh at/with them...

Richie - Well there's the tale of drunken anarchy at the Newcastle International launch... or my new story about John Smart presenting a blank board to a client in a kind of Emperors New Clothes way... or setting the land speed record for Dublin to Kilkenny in the dark with Toby navigating... the list goes on.

Ian - One of the most refreshing places I've had to work, where innovation and change are not dreaded but are a mere fact of everyday life.

Bernie - In the early days, trying to conduct a meeting in the first office with a client, whilst a 'senior' founding member of staff audibly threw up in the toilets following an enthusiastic liquid lunch.

Leaving a client dinner in a Cheshire country hotel for some fresh air (worse for wear), going for a quick stroll down a country lane, getting lost, it started raining heavily, a couple of hours passed - still lost, falling over into a hedge, cutting my face, ripping my tuxedo and whilst struggling to my feet, waving an on-coming local police car down. Unable to remember the name of the hotel, being driven around the area until I recognised it and jumping out, thanking them as if it was a local cab company. Convinced I would get the sack or lose the client, I was slightly nervous explaining to Doug and to the client at breakfast the next morning why I had disappeared and why my face looked like I had slept on a cheese grater. Incidentally, I didn't get the sack, the story strengthened my relationship with the client (with whom we were in our early days) and the relationship is still going strong.

Any night out with Mike in attendance - too numerous to mention.

Helen - My first outing at Navyblue as a Junior to the Ben Barrel Ball at Prestonfield house! Jon knows the rest!

Ray - Once upon a time...

Delia - I have a good laugh with my colleagues but at the same time we all work very professionally/heads down sort of thing.

Dave - Sorry couldn't think of one, didn't give myself enough time.

Jen - How old I felt when I discovered that one of the Directors is younger than me!

Nick - Are you sitting comfortably? Once upon a time... no I'm no good at stories.

Bart - Our MD used to party with pop singers on his rooftop terrace, chose his wife on an underwear shoot…still likes a boogie.

Justin - I don't have a best friend. I like to spread my love around.

Mark - Karl going to hospital with food poisoning after the Xmas party.

Malcolm – My best friend would rather drink copious amounts of beer, than hear about work!

Caroline B - I tell my friends when we win any new accounts like SFA, Ocean Terminal, Body Shop.

Craig - There I was standing knee high in water on Portobello beach. One hand holding a microphone and the other holding a ladder as the snow began to fall. www.tuneup.org.uk

Natalie C - No way, what goes on tour, stays on tour...

Rachel - We don't see each other very often, so try not to talk about work.

Jane - John Smart break-dancing at the Christmas party…

Rosie - The taxi queue story!

John S - The one about the blank boards.

Gavin - Mad, wacky but never boring.

Liza - It's a cool place to work with great, friendly people, lots of caffeine and plenty of banter - what more could you ever wish for?

Stuart - How good it is to work with a great bunch of people compared to other places I have worked.

Jonathan H - I just started a new job with a top design consultancy.

Paul - Plenty. They are all good.

Most memorable moment(s) in your life?

Doug - A stunning lady stepping off a National Express bus in St. Andrew Square, she is now my wife! The birth of my daughter Mia and my son Oli.

Karl - Being on Blind Date and meeting Cilla Black and, of course, being asked to work at Navyblue.

Jane - Jumping out a plane at 15,000ft over volcanoes in New Zealand.

Pete - Falling in love, getting married, birth of my son and a few things that I would never commit to paper.

Geoff - My first visit to London, can't remember the year but Jaws had just come out (for the first time!) and people were queuing around the block. A car crash where I was nearly a 'goner' but thankfully lived another day. Marriage, births and deaths are hugely impactful. Trips abroad for the first time, usually heat and smell rate most memorably. Facing 60+ Navyblue employees at the Christmas party.

Natalie M - There are too many, going on a date to Wimbledon Centre Court on a beautifully sunny Saturday (it worked, I married my date!), getting married, swimming with dolphins.

Mike L - To date, probably the last 5 months - the lifetime of my daughter. Until you become a parent it's difficult to imagine how rewarding it is.

Caroline T - There are numerous, so lucky when I look back on my life to have had such a rich life. Growing up in Kenya in a truly multicultural, multiracial, multilingual and immensely diverse country scenically, spiritually, culturally, economically.

This really set me up for life, appreciating and valuing difference amongst people rather than being afraid of difference. Travelling around the world, competing with my horse, boating on the West Coast of Scotland, studying and practicing Hellerwork. All the people who have influenced me and inspired me.

Toby - I can't even begin to narrow it down from things that have happened so far and I'd like to think there are plenty yet to come.

Jon - The births of my two kids, an unbelievable experience that everyone should have the pleasure of! Seeing my hometown team gain promotion to the top flight of English football for the first time ever. (A moving experience that only a true football fan will understand and appreciate - when you are introduced to something at the age of 2, it is in your blood!) Invited to judge the DSVC awards in Dallas. The first person outside the USA to have the honour.

Clare - Good... I would have to say when I was around 10 just doing whatever I wanted... dashing around on my diamond back, playing skat and generally arseing around with mates without anything to care about other than my dad telling me I couldn't wear a mix of green and orange illumino terry towlin' socks in the lounge bar of our pub where I grew up! Bad... Our pet Great Dane dying before I went to school and Mum telling me she'd be ok... she wasn't! Doing the bottling up wasn't great either!

Colin - Birth of first daughter 3 months premature, Hearts winning the Scottish Cup, wedding day, not in this order?

Richie - When after 2 weeks of plucking up the courage to chat Suzanne up, she said yes to a drink after work. The rest - as they say is history.

Ian - The birth of my 2 sons and my wedding day (I have to say that don't I?)

Bernie - Predictably my wedding day and witnessing the birth of my baby daughter.

Helen - First year at Uni, not having a care in the world and partying like its 1999 and living under the same roof as all my bestest mates. Meeting my soul mate 'Dave'. Getting a First Class Degree.

Delia - The birth of Amy.

Andy I - Getting married was kinda memorable.

Dave - Climbing Kilamanjaro (not sure of the spelling).

Jen - Sleeping outdoors in a swag in Australia during a thunderstorm, birth of my nephew.

Nick - (in this order)
- Meeting Annwen
- 06.42am 23.05.2003 Jake was born
- Watching 2 fighting gemsbok in the Kalahari National Park - there was absolute silence apart from the cracking sounds of horns.

Ray - Going to see Harry Potter at the flicks.

Bart - Scoring (football and with Jac, not necessarily in that order!!)

Mark - X-rated so can't disclose.
Justin - Saturday 30th August 2003. Everything that happened that day was f***king brilliant.

John D - Convincing the pilot of a plane (who was about to depart for Los Angeles) to stop and let me off because I was missing my wife.

Malcolm - Falling for Hazel and hearing God Save the Queen for the first time (Sex Pistols).

Caroline B - Every moment is special!

Craig - Paris, graduation and seeing my work in print!

Natalie C - Getting into art college and then getting my first 'real' job.

Rachel - Buying a home with Paul, living in Canada, all of my University years...

Rosie - Getting married, working in Australia and getting the ferry to work everyday past the harbour bridge & opera house in the sunshine - fab.

John S - Seeing Santa coming into my bedroom when I was 3 and realising it was my Dad. FA Cup Semi-Final at Hillsborough. Having my new baby girl dangled in front of me and hearing her first little squeak. Sitting on the ferry across the Cook Strait in New Zealand and feeling like my life was just about to start. I had a real 'moment'!

Gavin - (1) Getting stuck in a wheely bin trying to compress grass... as the next door neighbour arrived... a psychiatrist. (2) Getting lost 2000 feet over Cumbernauld and causing two shuttles to be diverted. (3) An honest diamond smuggling venture! But mostly finding a purpose in life...

Liza - Glen proposing on the top of Arthur's seat - tres romantic and graduating from uni.

Stuart - Rangers winning 9 in a row.

Jonathan H - Celtic stopping Rangers winning 10 in a row. But most importantly the birth of my son Reece and marrying Paula.

Paul - The first time I flew a plane from take off to landing without my instructors help.

Any other comments:

Gavin - Its only just begun!